While God lovingly and carefully creates each one of us in His image, He leaves a special, unique imprint that makes us wonderfully different. Yet parents often believe that the fairest way to raise children is to treat each one the *same*.

Barbara Sullivan states, "The problem is that we are dealing with individuals and what works with one child will most likely fail with another. It is the recognition of each child as an individual with definite needs and potential that is the aim of this book. While I offer no pat formulas, we will see that, indeed, no two children in any one family are alike, and different personalities require different parental guidance."

In *No Two Alike*, Barbara Sullivan shows you that while all children deserve to be loved equally, they need to be raised individually, with an awareness of the special needs of their birth order. This mother of four addresses the needs of each — from the responsible child to the "black sheep" of the family — alerting parents to potential problem areas and suggesting practical do's and don't's. *No Two Alike* offers the vital biblical insight parents need for raising the secure, productive, and happy children God intended them to be.

NO TWO
Alike

BARBARA SULLIVAN

Published by
√ chosen books

FLEMING H. REVELL COMPANY
OLD TAPPAN, NEW JERSEY

Scripture quotations identified NAS are from the *New American Standard Bible*, copyright © The Lockman Foundation 1960, 1962, 1963, 1968, 1971, 1972, 1973, 1975, 1977; NIV, *The New International Version*; RSV, the *Revised Standard Version*; ML, *The Modern Life Bible*; LB, *The Living Bible*; and KJV, The *King James Version* of the Bible.

ISBN 0-8007-9107-x

To my mother
who taught me that motherhood
is not a duty to be fulfilled
but joy, delight, and the highest
calling in life.

Contents

Contents

NO TWO
Alike

One

Unprepared Parenthood

It was a picture-perfect summer day in Michigan—warm enough to be relaxing, but not hot enough to be uncomfortable. My sister, Jeannie, and I, together with our children, had been enjoying the first month of vacation in our family's summer home.

For weeks, my nine-year-old daughter Shannon had been begging me to give her a permanent, and today I finally found the time to do it. When I removed the last curler and combed out her hair, Shannon was thrilled with the transformation in her looks. As she fluffed out her brand-new curls I realized gratefully that I had an hour to spare before time to start dinner. Perhaps I could stretch out on the sun deck with a good book.

Suddenly the peaceful afternoon was shattered by cries of pain. In a moment, the screen door banged open, admitting my sister and my eight-year-old son, Tom. Jeannie's hands were firmly grasping Tom's head and blood was streaming through her fingers.

"Don't get excited!" Jeannie yelled at me, knowing my horror of blood. "Go into the other room while I clean out the wound." Jeannie had been a surgical nurse and her tone carried authority. In this situation I was happy to let my little sister take charge, and I quickly vacated the kitchen. Shannon followed me into the family room where we sat on orange bean-bag chairs like expectant fathers in the waiting room.

"Head wounds always bleed a lot," Jeannie shouted for my encouragement. "It probably won't even require stitches."

Tom's howls gradually subsided, and in a few minutes Jeannie brought her much-subdued nephew into the family room to show me the newly cleaned wound. I took a deep breath and forced myself to look. . . . No, it wasn't nearly as bad as the profusion of blood seemed to indicate.

I found out that Tom had been having a forbidden sand battle and one of the little boys threw a metal object. After reassuring myself that he was going to survive, I gave him a brief lecture and dismissed him. He went running off to display his war wound to his friends.

Peace was restored to the day, and I was able to enjoy a few minutes alone on the porch, though too quickly it was time to fix supper.

"Shannon," I called, "come and help me get the kitchen cleaned up before dinner."

When Shannon finally answered my summons, it was obvious that her joy in the new permanent had evaporated. On her face was an expression that I had always interpreted as rebellion. Annoyed by her seeming lack of gratitude and her uncooperative attitude, I was on the verge of issuing a sharp rebuke when I remembered something from earlier in the week. I had been teaching a course on "parenting" to a group of women at the local church and challenged them to pray for wisdom before correcting their children. Now the Holy Spirit brought my words back to challenge me.

All right, Lord, I prayed silently. *Please give me the wisdom I need to deal with this situation.*

Stifling the irritation produced in me by the look on her face, I began to give Shannon her assignments in the kitchen. Suddenly, a question popped into my mind.

"Shannon, what are you feeling right now?"

Her answer came without a moment's hesitation: "Rejection."

"Rejection? Why are you feeling rejected?"

"Because it was our special day—you know, with the permanent and all. Now, Tom's ruined it. When he came in you forgot all about me."

Suddenly, I saw the day through her eyes and realized with a twinge of guilt that I had seen the perm only as a duty to be fulfilled. To her it was our "special" time together, a reinforcement of my love for her.

"Oh, Shannon, I'm sorry! I didn't realize this meant so much to you. We'll plan another special day that won't get ruined." I gave her a big hug for extra reassurance.

Shannon didn't reply but the smile on her face told me, in a language clearer than words, that my prayer for wisdom had been answered and soon after we had another special day.

Facing the Faces

Later I was able to give more thought to what had happened. Except for the prompting of the Holy Spirit, I would have reacted negatively to what I viewed as Shannon's rebellion instead of responding to her need for reassurance.

I remembered a remark made by my friend Faith when we were talking about the discipline of children. She explained her reluctance to punish her children by saying, "I can't handle their faces."

At the time that statement both amused and puzzled me.

When I laughingly asked her what she meant, she replied, "Well, you know. . . . They just get that certain look on their faces and I can't handle it."

Yes, I did know. What is there about "that certain look" that arouses a parent's anger or causes him (or more often, her) to shrink back from a confrontation? How was I to know how to handle that look? Somehow it triggered in me all the guilt, insecurity, and inadequacy I have ever felt as a parent. And I wondered how many times I had scolded my four children for what I thought they were thinking.

Raising a family in today's world is a frightening and challenging task. It is not surprising that many parents feel overwhelmed by it, or that more and more young couples make the decision not to have children. My children, during their grade school years, were exposed to temptations I had never heard of in college. Drugs are abundantly available, even for small children. Smoking pot is more acceptable now than smoking cigarettes was when I was in high school. When I was growing up, sex before or outside of marriage was a scandalous exception; today it is the rule, and young people who choose chastity are, at best, considered weird.

It used to be that success was assured for young people who worked hard in school and prepared themselves for a job in the field of their choice. No longer. Many college graduates—some with multiple advanced degrees—have discovered that largely because of the job shortage, society has no place for them. Hanging over the whole world is the threat of extinction—either through pollution or nuclear war. Is it any wonder that young people without Christ grab for any thrill they can find?

In the face of this seemingly hopeless situation, all of us—mothers and fathers alike—may as well admit that we are intimidated, not only by "that look" on children's faces, but also by the awesome responsibility entailed in bringing children into this world. We may well wonder if our efforts as parents will have any effect on our children in the face of the tremendous pressures they will face.

Yet Dr. Ross Campbell, Christian psychiatrist, found that "the home is stronger than any other influence in determining how happy, secure and stable a teenager is; how he relates to adults, peers, or children; how confident he is in himself; and how he responds to new or strange situations. Regardless of the many distractions in the life of a teenager, *the home has the deepest influence on his life*"[1] (italics mine).

So, since the home environment is vitally important, how does a Christian parent learn all the intricacies of child-rearing? When do we spank, when do we encourage, when do we set limits, and when do we release? So much of parenthood is trial and error but there are human lives and futures at stake. Courses on "Prepared Parenthood" are rare, and the ones that exist usually concentrate on the birth process, perhaps with some attention to the care and feeding of infants. Men and women bring many different skills into a marriage, but parenting is seldom one of them.

Psychology has been a mixed blessing. It has brought us great insights into the dynamics of the family but left us feeling that our failure at a crucial point in the child's life may keep that child from ever achieving his potential. As a result, we are easily intimidated by our children. We look for formulas that will ensure success.

The problem is that we are dealing with individuals and what works with one child will most likely fail with another. It is the recognition of each child as an individual with definite needs and potential that is the aim of this book. While I offer no pat formulas, we will see that, indeed, no two children in any one family are alike, and different personalities require different parental guidance.

It is interesting that while no two children in a family are alike, each of those children will assume one of several typical personality roles. These same roles occur in almost every family and vary from "the agreeable child" to "the black sheep." And often we parents respond to that child not as an individual, but in terms of this role.

Most often the role is tied in to a particular birth order. Frequently, for instance, the oldest child assumes the role of the responsible child and has needs that are much different from, say, the emotional youngest child.

Since different birth orders produce different personalities, we will examine the special needs and problems of each birth order, signs to alert you to a potential problem, practical do's and don't's, and the possible spiritual gifts of each child in the family constellation. We will look at our children in the light of the Bible's teaching, scientific research and testing, counseling and pastoral experiences my husband and I have had as leaders of a church fellowship, our trials as parents of four children, and valuable lessons learned by other parents as well.

We will see why our children are the way they are and how we can help them be the best they can be, for in spite of the feeling of hopelessness in the world around us, we can still have the deepest impact on our children. This is both reassuring and threatening, since most of us may as well admit that we are totally unprepared for our role as parents. Having made this admission, though, we can confess our lack of wisdom to God, who "gives generously to all without finding fault" (James 1:5, NIV) and ask Him to lend us His wisdom and love and authority as we endeavor to bring our children up "in the nurture and admonition of the Lord" (Ephesians 6:4, KJV). I think He's been wondering when we were going to get around to that.

Two

Authority: How Do We Handle It?

The authority and responsibility we have as parents to guide and direct a child's life is awesome. Jesus, after pointing to a little child as an example of humility, adds, ". . . Whoever causes one of these little ones who believe in me to sin, it would be better for him to have a great millstone fastened round his neck and to be drowned in the depth of the sea" (Matthew 18:6, RSV). Jesus' remark is a fearful warning not to put stumblingblocks in the way of new believers and especially in the lives of our children. No wonder so many of us Christian parents have a deep-rooted fear that we are inadequate for the responsibility of parenthood. But we can take comfort in the fact that God would not hold us responsible for the lives of our children without giving us the wisdom to direct them.

Authority—Some Mistakes

Of all our God-given abilities to use in rearing our children, I feel one of the most important areas for parents to understand is that of authority. Proper execution of authority can be learned and *must* be learned if we are going to understand our children's needs and meet them. Here is an overview of four mistakes parents make, and ways to change them into the rightful authority invested in us by God.

Power Play

Frequently, out of our feelings of inadequacy, we parents assert our authority in illegitimate ways. One of the most common is the power play.

How often have you said to your child: "Change your attitude" (without taking time to find out what the child's attitude is); or "Listen, young man, don't you dare look at me that way" (because when he does, he arouses your deep feelings of inadequacy as a parent); or "I'll give you one minute to do what I tell you!" (you don't know what you're going to do when the minute is up, but you're stalling for time); or "Don't you dare talk back to me!" (you have a bad enough opinion of yourself as it is); or "You don't need a reason; just do it because I said so" (and because you don't have a reason to give)?

The effect of such responses is to breed more rebellion in our children. Paul recognized this danger when he admonished fathers (and he could have included mothers) not to provoke their children to anger, but to "bring them up in the discipline and instruction of the Lord" (Ephesians 6:4, RSV).

Faced with a parent's unyielding display of superior power, the child has only two options: rebel or acquiesce. If he rebels, he has begun a pattern of behavior that will take him further and further away from his parents. If he acquieces, it is usually at the cost of "stuffing" his rebellious feelings inside himself. These repressed feelings often do more damage in later life, mentally and physically, than overt rebellion. And while they may cause a child to change behavior outwardly, the problem can continue to grow inwardly and may take years to surface.

One such case is Alice, a woman I know, who was fifty-two years old before she realized that she was a jealous person. The revelation was not only painful but unbelievable. All her life she told herself that one of her best qualities was her lack of jealousy toward those who seemed more favored by fortune. The revelation of intense feelings of jealousy caused her to ask the Holy Spirit why she had repressed it for so many years.

The next day, in the midst of cleaning her oven, she suddenly remembered an incident that occurred when she was three years old. She had been expressing some normal sibling jealousy toward her younger sister when her mother responded in a way that left Alice feeling condemned. She told Alice harshly that it was a "shame to be jealous." To emphasize the point, she repeated it several times. "It's a shame to be jealous" was a stern refrain deeply etched in Alice's mind. From that moment on, Alice's response was to deny any jealous feeling because she wanted to please her mother and because it was such a shameful thing. Since she did not know the right way to respond to jealous feelings, she suppressed them. It was only the power of the Holy Spirit that enabled Alice years later to see her hidden jealousy and repent of it.

The ultimate power play for parents is child abuse. This has increased greatly over the last few years probably as the stress of parenting has increased. In fact, more children now die at the hands of their parents than are killed by polio, whooping cough, tuberculosis, measles, diabetes, rheumatic fever, and hepatitis all combined.

The parent who knows he has God-given authority does not have to prove it by the power play. Proverbs 15:1 says that "a gentle answer turns away wrath, But a harsh word stirs up anger" (NAS). Rather than meeting your children's resistance with a superior display of power and a raised voice, you can speak softly but firmly with the authority God Himself has given you. In this way you won't become engaged in a shouting match in which you are on the same level as your child. The parent who tries to overcome his child with shouting and anger may win a temporary battle but will lose his child's respect. If you can understand that God has given a little bit of His authority to you to guide and direct your children, you won't have to prove your authority— just learn to exercise it. Everybody, even a child, respects authority when it is wielded with gentleness and firmness.

The Ostrich Ploy

How do some parents play ostrich instead of dealing with their feelings of inadequacy? They bury their heads in the sand, so to speak, and hope that somehow the kids will grow up with a minimum of direction and discipline. Instead of using their authority to guide and direct their children, they do not make the effort.

A good example of this refusal to discipline is the Old Testament figure Eli. Although he was the high priest and judged Israel for forty years, his two sons "were worthless men; they did not know the Lord" (1 Samuel 2:12, NAS). Although Eli knew his sons were doing wicked things, he did not try to correct them. For this reason, God said He would judge Eli's house "because his sons brought a curse on themselves and he did not rebuke them" (1 Samuel 3:13, NAS). Eli's sons were killed in battle, cut off in the prime of their lives. In the same manner, to the extent that we refuse to discipline our children, to that extent we diminish the quality of their lives.

My friend Betsy and her two children, ages seven and five, once spent a week with us. One day the younger child ran into the house crying because his big sister would not give him a turn on the big wheel. Betsy dismissed him with a wave of her hand.

"You two settle your own arguments," she told him. "Don't try to drag me into the middle."

It took all the self-control I possessed, together with a "don't say it" look from my husband, to keep me from blurting out to my friend, "But you're the mother; that's part of your job." I could have told her, too, the reason for her ostrich-like behavior. Betsy had been the youngest in her family, the spoiled darling of her parents. Even in adulthood she continued in the role of a child and refused to assume her rightful responsibilities as a mother.

Dr. John F. McDermott has written a fine book on sibling rivalry, appropriately titled, *Raising Cain (And Abel Too)*. In it, he gives parents this advice: "Fighting between brothers and sisters is fierce in the first four or five years of life. Then, you must settle conflicts for them. . . . But if you ignore the rivalry that comes with having two or more children, your kids may stay locked in battle with each other and even extend their hostilities to the outside world, to their relationships with others, as a way of life."[1]

Unfortunately, this prophecy proved true in Betsy's family. Her two children, now almost grown, have no relationship with each other, and the younger child is an angry, rebellious teenager.

Another case in point is that of Brian's mother, an only child, who was totally unprepared for the normal give and take of sibling rivalry. Unable to cope with the conflict among her six active children, she chose to ignore it. The result was the establishment of a "pecking order" in which the older children picked on the younger ones. Only Brian, the youngest, had no one on whom he could safely vent his hostilities. His teacher reported that he often arrived at school with scratch and bite marks on his face and arms, which he said came from his brothers and sisters. Now in the ninth grade and a poor student, Brian has been diagnosed through a series of psychological tests as emotionally rather than mentally retarded. He is another casualty of a mother's "playing ostrich" instead of assuming her responsibility as a disciplinarian for her children.

There is probably no aspect of child-rearing that is more aggravating that the constant bickering among children. There were times when I pretended not to hear what was going on in the family room in the hope that the children would settle the conflict themselves. It never happened. Sooner or later there was the inevitable "smack" of a hand contacting another child and then the screaming for "Mom!" began in earnest. There was no escaping it. I was the arbitrator and judge, whether I wanted to be or not. This is how children learn and if we do not help them settle their conflicts when they are small, they will never be ready for the give and take of the classroom or new friendships.

In my position as referee I gave each of my four children a drawer in which to keep very personal items. No other child was allowed to go through another's things or use any of the toys, crayons, or coloring books that belonged exclusively to someone else. Anyone who violated this rule was punished, usually by having to yield up the right to one of his special items. In this way, they learned early in life to respect the property of others, and that punishment would follow the violation of a household law. Children function better and feel more secure when given rules. Of course when the children are little, the rules have to be few and simple, such as, all toys must be put away before bedtime or there will be no stories read aloud. The mother who establishes clear rules of discipline in the house will find she has to spend less time acting as an arbitrator because the children will understand that when they have violated a rule they will be punished.

Abdication

Some mothers hope to escape their feelings of inadequacy by working outside the home. I am not talking about those mothers who have to work to survive financially but those who are unsure of themselves and opt for the extras their salaries will provide as a substitute for the nurturing they don't know how to give.

Dr. Arnold Tobin, a physician at Michael Reese Hospital in Chicago, found that between birth and sixteen months of age, there is a particular relationship between mother and child known as an "empathic tie"[2] commonly called bonding. The most characteristic feature of the empathic tie is that while mother and baby are emotionally close, the infant uses this closeness for support as he tests his own autonomy and learns to manage his own surroundings. If a mother spends too much time away from the infant and leaves him constantly in the care of multiple sitters during these crucial sixteen months, this bond is not formed. Dr. Tobin's research connected the lack of bonding with teen violence and suicide later in life. Even if the results are not this extreme, the lack of bonding will affect the child emotionally throughout his life.

These mothers must realize that there is no trade-off where human lives are at stake. As parents, we bear the responsibility before God for our children. He has entrusted them to us and given us some of His authority to raise them. This is where our sense of security and identity as a mother comes from.

Fathers, too, often use their work and the necessity of making a living as an excuse for abdicating their parental responsibilities. The man's traditional role is that of breadwinner, and it is not surprising that many fathers see material support as their most important contribution to the family.

Until recently, many psychologists believed that a warm, supporting mother was all that was needed to produce well-adjusted children. New research appears to indicate that it is the father who plays the most important role not only in helping his children feel secure in their sexual identities but also in being successful in life. Psychologist Lis Hoffman, after reviewing research in this area, concluded:

From our data, it would appear that a mother's love and attention makes a boy feel warm and cozy, but a father's equips him to face the world. For example, both lead to a feeling of being loved and accepted, but a positive father relationship is associated with a high degree of self-confidence with respect to abilities, while a positive relationship with the mother is associated with a low degree of self-confidence . . .

I can sum up and say that, in this study, we found that when the father is more powerful than the mother, disciplines his children, and has a warm companionship with them, the boys—and to a lesser extent the girls—will have self-confidence and feel accepted by others, show a positive assertiveness in the peer-group, have skills, like others, be well-liked, and exert influence.[3]

Mothers actually tend to make their children introverted. They are apt to help the growing child focus on his feelings and needs and also to consider other people from this perspective. This is valuable training but, without the balancing influence of a strong male figure to help the child become more extroverted, his personality may not develop fully. It is the relationship with the father that turns the child away from himself and outward to the world. Studies show that a child raised without a relationship with a father figure tends to be too introspective and without self-esteem. Fathers need to be more than the "meal ticket" if children are going to be successful in finding their place in the world and the Kingdom of God.

Parental Prophecies

Because of the tremendous authority that parents have, our words have great power to set the direction of our children's lives. As parents we want all of our children to develop fully in the talents and gifts God has given them, so we must be careful not to short-circuit that development by negative statements. It is not uncommon for parents, knowingly or unknowingly, to speak prophecies over their children which then bind those children into undesirable patterns of behavior.

A case in point is that of a young woman named Amon, who came to the United States from Thailand when she was thirty years old. Two years later, she accepted Christ and joined our fellowship. In her public prayers, she often told God that she wanted to "be a good girl." Not until she came to talk to me about a problem did I understand what was behind that deep cry of her heart.

In Thailand, she told me, there is a superstition that a child born on Sunday who does not have curly hair will have a "curly" (crooked or devious) heart. Amon was born on Sunday—and her hair is straight. While she was growing up, both her mother and her aunt frequently reminded her of this superstition. After one such reminder, she got on her bike and rode for miles, crying all the while.

The belief that she had been destined forever to be an evil person gave Amon a deep feeling of unworthiness. To combat this, she tried hard to be good. After she went to work, she lived a simple lifestyle and spent all her extra time and money helping her widowed mother and her younger brothers and sisters. When she became a Christian, Amon continued in the serving, giving role, but she was unable to receive anything from others.

After she told me her story, I suggested that we pray together and break what was, in effect, a curse that had been put on her life by the superstitious prophecy of her mother and aunt. As we prayed, she actually began to sob as the Holy Spirit set her free from having lived under this lie for so many years. Since then she has come into a new freedom, she is even able to say no to the the many demands of her family. She can now separate those things she believes God wants her to do from the things she used to do to try to be "good."

Amon is an example of a child who has been bound by an obviously lethal parental prophecy. We parents may not speak in such extreme terms, but some things we tell our children can be just as damaging:

"You are so lazy, you'll never amount to anything."

"You never pay attention."

"Can't you do anything right?"

"You are such a slob!"

"Why are you always so crabby?"

"You're just like your father" (or "your aunt" or "your grand-mother"—anyone who can be held up to the child as an obvious example of some undesirable trait).

The Israelites were a people familiar with the power of parental prophecies. The patriarch of the family always gave a blessing or prophecy over his sons. At the end of Jacob's life, he called his twelve sons together and said: "Assemble yourselves that I may tell you *what shall befall you* in the days to come" (Genesis 49:1, NAS, italics mine). Jacob knew that what he prophesied would come to pass because of his position of authority as the father and head of the family. As parents, given by God the authority and responsibility to direct our children's lives, our words have pro-phetic effect.

We Christians should know that words have power. By His Word, God created the heavens and the earth and all things in them. We, too, have power to create with our words either good or bad character traits in our children. Ask the Holy Spirit to reveal to you any undue control your words may have placed on one of your children—perhaps in infancy or early childhood—and then break that control by revoking those words in the name of Jesus. Otherwise that child, like Amon, may live for years under the handicap imposed by your prophecy.

We can speak constructive statements that will bring out pos-itive characteristics in our children. I first saw the truth of this in my daughter Shannon's life when she was in the sixth grade. She and several friends were going to exclude one girl from an outing downtown. Rather than berate her for her lack of charity, I had the inspiration to say, "Shannon, I know you are going to invite

Cindy because you are too kindhearted not to." With that I rested my case.

The next day when Shannon came home from school, she told me: "You sure were right, Mom."

"About what?" I questioned.

"About my being too kindhearted to exclude Cindy. I invited her to go with us today."

Since God has given us the power of creativity, let us be sure that we create good character traits in our children. We need to be acquainted with the special qualities in each of our children so that we can call them forth at appropriate times.

Rightful Authority

While the father is the head of the home and carries tremendous authority to set the direction for his child's life, I believe the mother has a special gift for intercession. Just as Jesus submitted to the Father and intercedes for each one of the Father's children (Hebrews 7:25), so the wife who is submitted to her husband has the authority to make intercession for her children. Women have great sensitivity to the Spirit of God and, because of their close relationship with their children by bonding, are especially tuned in to the needs of each child.

Intercession

God demonstrated to me the power we mothers have as intercessors one afternoon as I was busy working on this book. A small child and her mother were visiting with my daughter Kelly in the kitchen. I was working in my study but the three-year-old kept running in to ask me questions. She was too cute to ignore, so I decided to go upstairs to my oldest child John's room where I could close the door and work undisturbed.

Soon after I sat down at his desk, I began to experience an unpleasant sensation. My heart began to beat faster, my palms grew sweaty, and I was having difficulty concentrating. I mentally reviewed what I had eaten for lunch an hour previously, thinking I might be having some sort of food reaction. I had eaten a very bland lunch and had not had any caffeine. By now I couldn't concentrate and decided to stop and pray.

As I was praying, I realized that I was having an attack of anxiety. As soon as I realized that, a thought slid into my mind: *This is what your son John felt every time he sat at this desk.* Instantly my mind was flooded with pictures of John sitting at this desk, his head bent over a book, studying night after night through his twelve years of grammar and high school. Now, for the first time, I realized the anxiety and pressure he felt all during those early years.

I began to cry and pray for him to be released from a spirit of anxiety. The longer I prayed, the deeper I sobbed. Gradually the feeling lifted and I felt the Holy Spirit had accomplished that release.

John was a freshman in medical school by this time and, although he felt he had conquered this anxiety, I learned later that the weeks leading up to my experience had been difficult for him. All the old anxiety and resultant mental blocks during tests had returned with a new intensity. He was beginning to feel he would never be free and was even questioning his future in medical school. After God allowed me to function as an intercessor for John by identifying with his problem, he was totally released from anxiety. Now, two years later, he is still amazed at his lack of anxiety, especially before tests.

A short time later another incident occurred that definitely convinced me of the power of maternal intercession. I was restless one night and kept tossing and turning in bed. I knew my husband had a long day of work ahead of him and I didn't want to keep him from sleeping, so I went into my son Tom's room. Tom was away at school and, as I climbed into his bed, I said a quick prayer for him.

As I lay there in the dark, still unable to sleep, I realized with a start that thoughts of suicide had begun to drift in and out of my mind. At first I refused even to acknowledge them but the attack became more pronounced. I was completely baffled until I realized I was in Tom's bed and a little warning voice inside me seemed to indicate Tom was in trouble.

I began to pray immediately in Jesus' name, asking Him to protect Tom from thoughts or demonic influences toward suicide. I even rebuked Satan and asked God to keep Tom from harming himself. For a period of time it almost seemed I was wrestling with the devil for my son's life. Eventually the attack subsided and a feeling of peace replaced my fear and anxiety. I finally was able to sleep.

I found out several days later that Tom had indeed been struggling with overwhelming thoughts of suicide during the time of my prayers. So, God again used me as an intercessor, this time to stand in the gap for Tom and help him overcome those thoughts.

God has given our children to us for a period of time to nurture and bring into a relationship with Him, but they are really His. As we use the authority and wisdom He has given us, we will find that intercessory prayer is our most powerful spiritual weapon.

Since these experiences, I have made it a practice to pray in each one of my children's rooms. It might be while I am changing the sheets, cleaning the room, or putting away clean clothes in the closet, but the whole time I am in there I intercede for that son or daughter. Often, God gives me a special insight into their needs as I pray.

Parents and Submission

Jesus had just entered Capernaum wher a centurion approached him asking Jesus to heal his servant. Jesus said that He would go and heal the servant but the centurion answered:

*Lord, I am not worthy for You to come under my roof, but just
say the word, and my servant will be healed.*

*For I, too, am a man under authority, with soldiers under me;
and I say to this one, "Go!" and he goes, and to another, "Come!"
and he comes, and to my slave, "Do this!" and he does it.*

Matthew 8:8–9, NAS

The centurion recognized a principle of authority that is vital
for parents: If we are to exercise our legitimate authority over our
children in a way that is constructive—restraining but not domineering and coercive—then we must be people who are also
under authority. Only those who are properly under authority
and respectful of that authority will be able to minister authority
properly to others.

If the mother is not respectful and submissive to her husband's
authority, she will not be able to have proper authority over the
children. She will either be domineering or unable to discipline
them. The father, likewise, must have a respectful attitude toward the authorities in his life such as his parents, his boss, and
all other governing authorities. We cannot expect our children to
have the proper attitude toward our authority if we have a dis-
paraging attitude toward authority ourselves. However, when,
like the centurion, we are properly related to authority, then we,
too, will be able to issue directives to those under our authority,
especially our children, and they will obey. Authority, properly
exercised, will not be too abusive or too lax, but will produce
self-disciplined children who will be able to achieve their potential in life.

Three

But I Treated Them All the Same

Several years ago, about a week before Thanksgiving, my son Tom telephoned to say he was driving home from college to talk to us about his schedule of courses for the following semester. Even though his school was only an hour-and-a-half away, he had not been home for a month.

The house seemed empty with three of my four children in college. John was a senior at the University of Illinois, Shannon a junior at Arizona State, and Tom a sophomore at Northern Illinois University. Only my fifteen-year-old daughter Kelly was living at home. It would be good to have more than three people at the dinner table again.

I was looking forward to seeing Tom, not only for the chance of feeding him a home-cooked meal, but also to reassure myself that everything was all right. Since the summer he had been moody and depressed, quite a change for my usually optimistic third child. I blamed it on his inability to decide on a major course of study. Since this was his second year, he needed to make that decision soon, and perhaps tonight we could help him.

After the dinner dishes were cleared and stacked in the dishwasher, Tom spread the scheduling materials on the kitchen table. He and his dad read tediously through every major course of study discussing the pros and cons of each. I sat listening, occasionally offering a comment. I had ample time to study Tom's face as he and John talked. He seemed distracted and tense and I wondered what had changed him from the happy-go-lucky boy he had been in high school.

After several hours, the schedule was completed and John stretched and was about to get up when Tom put a restraining hand on his arm.

"Wait a minute, Dad. There's something else I want to talk about."

Tom paused for a minute and his face looked white and pinched. I sat there, holding my breath, almost afraid to hear what he was about to say.

"I've been doing drugs for about six months. I've used a lot of my college money for cocaine and I don't know if I am able to stop."

My first reaction was disbelief—*not my son!*—but deep down I knew it was true. Of course, this was the reason for the depression and moodiness. How subtly I had ignored what I didn't want to face; I should have recognized the symptoms. My husband, a full-time practicing dentist, and I have pastored a church that began in our home thirteen years ago. The past three years we have worked with a state drug rehabilitation center and I was quite familiar with drug effects. Tom's behavior was classic.

The next few days I experienced an outpouring of emotions: I was praising God or yelling at Him; loving Tom deeply or hating him for what he was doing; seeing a vision of victory in God or feeling overcome with evil. In the midst of soul-searching and overwhelming guilt, I heard myself ask the same question many different ways: Why Tom? I treated them all the same, didn't I ? I tried to give them all the same love and attention. What went wrong?

The next month was a real learning experience for the whole family. We realized that Tom needed our love and support but also had to repent and take responsibility for his own life. There was a divine tension between these two needs as we learned to walk in the balance. I learned how to pray with more effectiveness and also discovered that I had some hidden anger at God. During Christmas vacation of that year, the hold drugs had on Tom's life was broken and God began to restore him. Now, three years later, he has continued to walk in that victory.

The problem was solved but the question that had plagued me remained: "Did I really treat them all the same?" I began to read and study and remember in the hope that what I learned I could pass on to other parents who, like myself, wanted to see each of their children develop to his fullest potential.

Exposing the Lie

As I looked back over my life I realized that I didn't, in fact couldn't, treat my four children the same. To begin with, each child's start in life was different. John, my oldest child, had only my husband and me to look to while Kelly, my youngest, was greatly influenced by her three older siblings. My husband and I were softened by each child and so we responded differently to the third and fourth children than to the first. One was less demanding than the others and so we had less anxiety over her than with the more difficult child, which affects the personalities of both.

And even if we parents were to succeed in treating all our children alike, there would still be differences in their own order and positions in the family. In fact, two oldest children from different families are usually more similar than the oldest and youngest of the same family.

Many parents, like myself, try to treat all the children alike because we believe that is the fair thing to do. I can remember my mother often saying proudly, "I treated all you children the same," and I'm sure in her mind she did. I attempted to carry on this noble ideal with my own children, but had to realize that to distinguish between them does not mean to show favoritism. Children may complain at first if they are not all given identical benefits or punishments, but if the parents make it clear that different people like different things and different ages require different punishment, the children will eventually realize that distinctions are not discriminatory.

But notice this important point: We may not treat our children all alike, but we must *love* all of them equally. We have an obligation to be fair and impartial, and as we will see next, we can start by helping them develop individually, by incorporating affirmation, and by applying birth-order principles.

The Importance of Individualization

Before my first child, John, reached his third birthday, he was the oldest of three children. For me, each day of coping with three babies was a struggle just to survive. It seemed to me that the only way I could retain my sanity and any semblance of order in the home was to lump them together in a group, instead of treating them as individuals.

In such situations, the aggressive child is always the one who gets the most attention, and the passive child is the one who gets the most neglect. In our family, Shannon was that passive child, serving as a sort of buffer between her two contending brothers. Because she was "good," she was neglected. I'm sure that is why she reacted so strongly to being pushed aside on her "special day" in chapter one—it was the story of her life. My failure to take the time to bring out her special gifts and talents caused her to remain locked into this passive position until she went away to college. Then, freed from her lifelong role of peacemaker, she

34

began to develop in areas where neither she nor her parents ever suspected she had talent. I thank God that His grace is covering my mistakes.

Dr. McDermott, pointing out that "a struggle for independence goes on between brothers and sisters," says that parents can minimize this sibling rivalry "by helping them differentiate from each other, become separate individuals. Then they don't have to fight so hard to get that independence."[1]

The importance of a parent's understanding the special gifts and talents of each child was emphasized in a twenty-year study of the behavorial development of 231 infants by Doctors Chess and Thomas. The results of their study stress the different temperaments of babies; they are "born different." Along with this, though, there is the interaction between a particular parent and particular child and the way they "fit" together that shapes a child. Dr. Chess, the author of the book *Your Child Is a Person*, says

> that the most significant factor in determining a child's destiny is not whether he is "easy" or "difficult." In fact, "difficult" infants . . . did not necessarily develop problems. The key was what Chess called "goodness of fit" between parents and baby. If the parent's expectations and demands of "fit" were in accord with the child's own capacities and style of behavior, then the baby enjoyed optimal development. If parents *didn't understand or appreciate a child's special qualities, problems occurred.* Surprisingly, even divorce or the death of a parent was not as important as this basic "fit"[2] (italics mine).

Only tremendous amounts of time, wisdom, and prayer can enable parents to recognize early the uniqueness of each child and help each one to develop his or her special abilities. This is one of the most important assignments of our lives as parents.

The Importance of Affirmation

In addition to recognizing the uniqueness of each child, parents need to affirm the value of each child. Because parents are people, it is not surprising that they find it easier to love—or at least to like—one child more than the other(s). Sometimes this affinity is more for a particular stage of development (babyhood, for example, or the toddler stage, or even in rare instances adolescence). Sometimes this affinity for a particular child alters as the children grow, and sometimes the mother is drawn to one child and the father to another through life.

The reasons for this (perhaps subconscious) favoritism are so varied and so subtle that it would be impossible to deal with all of them, but two of the more obvious ones are (1) a child's acceptance or rejection of the parent's values and (2) the parent's sex preference.

Differing Values

Before I became a Christian, intellectual ability was my most important measure of value. It seemed to me that this was the key to all success and happiness in life. My oldest child, John, was a straight A student and became the preferred child—the role model for his siblings. I didn't express this preference in so many words, but the other children picked it up in my treatment of John and my praise for his report cards. They had different gifts, talents, and motivation, and they ended up feeling inferior to their older brother.

After my husband and I came to a living, deep faith in Christ, our value system underwent an abrupt change. Now we saw spiritual values as more important than worldly values; a straight A report card was not as important as character qualities like kindness and faith. This change was jolting to John who, besides having the achievement-oriented nature of the first-born, had been trained to think of intellectual success as the most important goal in life. Even as a college student, John was still torn between the goals of intellectual achievement and his desire to serve God. It was a struggle for him to decide if his ambition to be a doctor was really God's will for him or based on his need to achieve what he perceived as his highest possible goal.

John's questions remained unanswered until the first day of medical school as he sat in a classroom. As the professor lectured, John told us later, he had a strong sense of purpose and knew that this was exactly what he was supposed to be doing. He felt assured that his motives were God-given.

Christian parents should be aware of the danger of showing preference to the child who conforms most closely to their values, especially their religion. Too often, outward conformity to a set of beliefs is not accompanied by an inner transformation. Gently, patiently, and by our example, we must convey to our children that Christ is the most important person in our lives. But at the same time we must show them that they are loved and accepted even when they reject our values.

Our oldest three children all went through a period in high school where—at least on the surface—they were in rebellion against the Christian faith. The most painful time was to see them sit defiantly with arms folded in church—especially since my husband was the pastor! I decided the pain came from my wounded pride and that was really not a good motive to use in disciplining them. Since my husband and I knew that we had truly given God first place in our lives and had given our children to Him, we had faith to believe that, sooner or later, He would bring them back into the fold (Matthew 7:17). And He did. I am thankful that God kept me from pressuring them into conformity during that time, in spite of my embarrassment at their behavior, because I know now that their faith is not an inherited one, but a gift each received personally from God.

I was sharing this information about my children's "rebellious stage" with some women during a weekend seminar. One of the women said she had pressured her oldest son to be a good, committed Christian. "And he was," she commented sadly, "for the first twenty years of his life. He read his Bible, sang in the choir, attended all the youth meetings, and set a good example for the young people. Now," she said in a quiet voice, "he is living with a woman who just found out she is pregnant, and he is a drug addict. If you had told me this would happen even two years ago, I would have laughed in your face. If I could do it over again, I sure wouldn't be so legalistic and demanding."

Basically, most children truly want to please their parents. If a child completely rejects his parents' values, it is usually because he senses that their values are false, or because he feels he can never win their love and approval. By depending on the Holy Spirit to touch those individual needs through us, we can avoid the pitfall of becoming controlling, overprotective, overdemanding parents. He will give us the wisdom to know when to let go and when to exhort them. The child will then have freedom to develop his own special gifts at his own rate. When he fails to live up to our standards and expectations, we must remember it is God's reputation that is at stake, not ours (Isaiah 48:11).

We need to reexamine our motives in disciplining our children. Are we concerned primarily with their looking good or with their becoming more like Christ? If our desire is to see the fruits of the Holy Spirit—love, joy, peace, and the rest—come forth in their lives, we will concentrate less on their actions ("Don't smoke; don't drink; study hard") and more on the inner attitudes of their hearts.

Preferences Based on Gender

On the occasion of my parent's fiftieth wedding anniversary, my father had a large celebration dinner. While we were at the door waiting to welcome the guests, I was standing between my father and my older brother, Tom. As the first couple entered the room, Dad greeted them and then reached in front of me to put his arm around my brother. "And this is our son, Tom," he said proudly.

As I stood behind them, I seemed for a moment to be suspended outside of time. At last I could see objectively what my subconscious mind had known all my life: My dad (and also my mother) preferred boys. This realization aroused no anger or resentment, but rather a sort of "eureka!" feeling that so many things had finally come into focus.

One of the things God had to deal with in me after I became a Christian was a deep rejection of my femininity that translated into fierce competitiveness. In my early life, I had been a tomboy. For several years I was the only girl on an all-male softball team. As a college student I enjoyed being the only girl in a pre-med curriculum. I relished the competition against men—especially when I set the curve on a test. With God's help, I finally learned to accept my femininity—even to delight in it—but I never understood why I had rejected it in the first place. Now, at last, I had been given that understanding.

My parents never consciously showed a preference for my brother—and they were, in fact, pleased that their second child was a girl. Like many others in our society, however, they held a basic belief that males have greater value than females. Some Christian teaching seems to propagate the theory that even God prefers men over women. This belief manifested itself in many areas, including that of education. Whereas my sister and I had to convince my dad that he would not be throwing money away by sending us to college, my brother had no choice: He had to go. I realize now that I myself have subconsciously held and conveyed to my children this same belief that boys have a greater purpose in life than girls.

Many parents, especially fathers, are secretly (or sometimes openly) disappointed if their first child is not a boy. If the second child is also a girl, she is often given the father's name or a feminine version thereof, in an attempt to alleviate his disappointment in her sex. Such a girl may grow up with a deep sense of rejection.

In matriarchal societies and families, on the other hand, it is women who are the dominant and preferred sex. In these instances, where the mother is the strong, domineering parent and the father is weak and henpecked, the male child may feel rejected and, in an effort to become accepted, may adopt feminine characteristics. It is widely acknowledged that this family pattern often produces homosexual tendencies in children.

One young woman in our fellowship grew up with a weak, henpecked father. She was a strong, achieving first-born girl and despised her father for his passivity. She married a man similar to her father and when her second child, a son, was born, transferred this same attitude of male inferiority to him. It was only as her son moved into his adolescent years and began having serious emotional problems that she realized what she had done. She had to forgive her father and ask forgiveness for her attitude of superiority, which was causing her son to feel rejected and despised.

To quote McDermott again, "Nothing is more potentially serious for distorting personality development (as well as complicating and intensifying sibling rivalry) than parents preferring one sex over the other. The child of the 'wrong' gender will feel disappointed in his or her sex, whichever it is."[3]

In order to affirm equally their children of both sexes, parents must not have any confusion about their own value and identity. While clearly defining the different roles of men and women, the New Testament makes it plain that "in the Lord woman is not independent of man, and man is not independent of woman" (1 Corinthians 11:11, ML). We are different in our roles but not in our personhood or value, just as Christ was equal to the Father, even though His role was subordinate. Only when we mothers and fathers truly understand our value to God will we be able to give our children the security of knowing how highly valued they are, both by God and by their parents.

Be Aware of the Birth-Order Factor

Too often we parents are unaware of the many variables affecting our offspring who are raised in the same family. Because we think all our children are nurtured in the same environment, we live under the false assumption that each one will respond in the same way as the first-born.

According to the eminent German psychiatrist Alfred Adler, there is an error in this thinking. "It is a common fallacy to imagine that children of the same family are formed in the same environment. Of course there is much which is the same for all children in the same home, but the psychological situation of each child is individual and differs from that of others, because of the order of their succession."[4] It is easy to see, for instance, that with each successive child the influence of the parents becomes less and that of the siblings becomes greater.

And taking this family positioning one step further, we find that birth order is directly tied in to personality patterns. As each child is born, he searches for a distinct role in the family, one that is different from the preceding children's. In time, this role becomes recognized by the child himself as well as by his brothers and sisters.

The oldest child often develops patterns of responsibility since he is first and followed by younger and more dependent siblings. The second child becomes sensitive to rejection as he subconsciously compares himself to the first-born, and seeks recognition by making himself agreeable. The third child has to find a new avenue of achievement and often turns away from the family to the community. This is just a microcosm of the process children go through to establish their identities. They will also be affected by physiological conditions, genetic inheritance, age and sex differences, family size, the disability or death of an older sibling, and the child's perception of his placement in the family. (These last factors are analyzed in my previous book, *First Born, Second Born*.)

41

Because of all these influences, each child in the family has different needs. The demands of the first child for love and approval are quite different than that of the second and the third, etc. Sometimes parents, in an honest attempt to deal fairly, try to give all of their children the same treatment. Such consistency will satisfy the needs of only one child. We must learn how to relate to the uniqueness of each child within the family constellation.

In the remainder of this book, starting in the next chapter with the oldest child and his responsible nature, we will be exploring the role that birth order plays in uniqueness. It is my prayer that, with the help of the Holy Spirit, parents will begin to understand and respond to the different needs built into each of the children God has given them.

Four

The Responsible Child

Michelle, normally a vigorous, active woman, had for most of her life been incapacitated, at intervals of about three weeks, by migraine headaches. This had been the week. In an effort to uncover some reason for the headaches, our Sunday night house group began asking Michelle questions and we saw that she became increasingly agitated as we probed into her childhood years.

"I was the oldest, the one who always had to be responsible. I stayed home and did the canning, watched the little boys, cleaned the house, and ironed the clothes," Michelle said, her voice becoming charged with emotion. "My younger sister, Elizabeth, always managed to disappear when there was work to be done, so I had to do her chores as well as mine. In spite of that, she was the one my parents loved the most. When she was fifteen, she was drowned. All I could think of was, *They would rather it had been me."*

With that statement, Michelle dissolved into tears. The other eleven members of our group sat silently, some praying and others watching Michelle and empathizing with her as the tears ran down her cheeks. Some of them may have been reliving similar hurts. No one spoke. We knew that our questions had uncovered an old wound, and that Michelle's tears needed to be shed. They had been repressed far too long.

In his position as leader of our house church, my husband, John, suggested that we gather around Michelle and ask God to set her free from resentment and the resultant headaches. He then instructed Michelle to release the responsibility of her family to God, and to forgive them for placing so much of the burden on her shoulders. Since Michelle had told us of several specific incidents in her past that were still painful, John had her mention each incident and forgive all the family members involved, naming each one of them. Finally, he had her ask God's forgiveness for her anger and thank Him that He had been in control of all the circumstances of her life. As I watched peace settle over Michelle's troubled features, I believed that her monthly bouts with headaches were finally over, and time proved that assumption correct.

To Much, Too Soon

Michelle is not an exception: She represents the striving, eager-to-please first-born who almost inevitably gets the brunt of responsibility from parents. This is true whether the first-born is a boy or a girl, though the particular responsibilities may differ. If the oldest child is a girl, she is usually expected to be "Mother's helper," both with the housework and with the younger children, a surrogate parent, and in-house baby-sitter. First-born girls with younger sisters, like Michelle, seem to have it particularly hard.

These grown-up first-borns are the women Wilson and Edington were addressing when they wrote,

> As the big sister in a two-girl family you had a problem: no matter how diligently or conscientiously you strove to shine forth as a model of mature and responsible behavior in a feckless world, you always felt upstaged by your little sister. Her more extroverted and careless approach to life almost invariably appeared to earn more rewards for her than your high standards were ever able to gain for you. When you were both children it must have often seemed to you that she was permitted to get away with murder—to flout many of the rules which you had so carefully learned and built into the very fabric of your personality.[1]

Dr. Lucille Forer, herself an oldest child, says that the oldest girl in a family often has migraine headaches in adult life.[2] Whereas the oldest boy, according to Dr. Forer, is more likely to "act out" the tension he feels, the oldest girl turns that tension inward and bears the consequences. In many cases, these consequences include headaches.

The oldest sister of a brother is in a somewhat better position since she has no immediate female rival, but she is still cast in a lifelong role of problem solver—the one that the others, including little brother, will depend on throughout life.

While the oldest girl may be overburdened with caring for younger siblings, the oldest son bears the responsibility of being the guardian and upholder of the family values and traditions. It is the first-born son who must validate the parents and be successful in school and career: He is the future president, doctor, bank president, or other prestigious position in life. Not only will he be successful academically but he will probably be athletic. All of his father's unfulfilled dreams will be realized in this first-born son.

Most mothers also desire a first-born son and, as a result, show him more attention. Because of this, first-born males rank highest in verbal skills, which later in life predisposes them to academic success.

While younger children in the family might tend to envy the amount of attention directed toward the oldest son, all the attention places considerable stress on him. What if he can't live up to their expectations? Also, the family frequently looks to the oldest son for emotional support: Mother often expects him to serve as surrogate husband and siblings may look on him as an alternate father. Later in life he will be the one called to handle family problems. My oldest brother is the one who took over the care of my mother's financial affairs after the death of my father. He calls my sister and me periodically to fill us in on specific details and to make suggestions. He has definitely become the head of the family. Often, the oldest child, like the only child, becomes the one who will look after the elderly parent or parents.

So, because parents rely on them to perform, the first child in a family is usually the one who is most responsible, the one who can be counted on to do what he is asked to do. And, as he or she responds, parents pile the most important tasks on his shoulders, giving more and more responsibility to the first child and less and less to the others. Knowing how many reminders and how much prodding it will take to get her later-born children to carry out their chores, the tired and busy mother finds it much easier to assign those chores to the responsible first-born. The unfortunate result is that the oldest child can become burdened with too much responsibility, while the younger children remain immature and irresponsible.

Pushed into too much responsibility too soon, the oldest child sometimes resembles a little old man or woman: serious, worried, sensitive, concerned with problems beyond his years. As Dr. Karl König, the author of *Brothers and Sisters*, has commented, the "first child is rarely able to experience the carefree wonder and beauty of childhood."[3] This early deprivation of the opportunity to be carefree has a lifelong effect, and many oldest children are never able to enjoy the wonders that our heavenly Father has put all around us. Like the elder brother of the Prodigal Son, they keep their faces pressed against the window of life, yearning to take part in the celebration going on inside but knowing their role is to work and never disobey. No surprise that the elder brother was "angry and refused to go in" (Luke 15:28, NIV). No surprise that Michelle had headaches caused by repressed anger.

During his freshman year in college my first-born son brought home a mug that read, "If I don't do it, it doesn't get done." We laughed about it, but deep down I was not really amused. I knew that this slogan was an expression of his deepest feelings, and that I was the one who had instilled this attitude in him.

Too often, the primary message that we parents convey to our first-borns is this: "You are the one who is responsible, you are the role model, all the younger children look to you: Don't let us down."

The Conformer

Why is it that so many parents give the lion's share of responsibility to their oldest children? Is it only because they are the oldest, or is it something inherent in the character of first-borns?

A responsible individual, according to Edith Neisser, is one who is concerned with the needs and welfare of others. "Those who are responsible," she says, "tend to be those who are also somewhat conscientious, conforming and competent. These qualities are prominent in many first children."[4]

My own first-born son affords a classic example of the oldest child's responsible nature. I have already mentioned the summer home in Michigan that our family enjoyed for a number of years. During our summers there, my dentist-husband joined us for weekends. On Sunday evening, before leaving to go back to the city, John would call our two boys together and assign them their chores for the week. Our first-born son, John, would immediately go to his room and write down the list of responsibilities he had been given. Then, as he completed each chore, he checked it off his list. Every Thursday afternoon about three o'clock—five hours before his father's usual time of arrival—our third-born, Tom, would ask me if I could remember what he was supposed to do.

The first-born's greatest desire is to please his parents. He grew up looking to them as his role models and seeking their approval for his actions. No one stood between him and his parents, and their high expectations for him gave him the desire to succeed. He tries to win their approval by copying their actions and especially their behavior and attitudes when disciplining him. He conforms to their standards and becomes, in effect, a miniature parent.

One way he finds he can please his parents is through his performance. After the birth of the second child, many first children go through a brief period of rebellion and anger toward their mothers for bringing the baby home. Eventually they realize that the quickest way to regain Mom's love and approval is by being obedient and responsible—by conforming to their parents' expectations. They learn to run and get the diaper for Mom, watch little sister when she is in the playpen, pick up the toys after dinner, and all the things that get Mom to say: "You are such a big help to me." He quickly learns that it is performance that counts.

It is natural that a child who is always expected to measure up to his parents' high standards will come to feel that what happens depends largely on his own efforts. A possible result, according to Karl König, is that "he may well develop a great deal of pride and an overbearing attitude in order to comply with the demands of his own high sense of responsibility."[5] The feeling that he is responsible for what happens helps to explain the "bossiness" so evident in many first children.

Since the first-born is the child most likely to excel in those characteristics valued by the family, the birth order of the parents will either modify or intensify the first child's tendency toward rigidity and perfectionism. The first child who has two first-born parents may be exceptionally tense, anxious, and achievement-oriented. First-born parents need to be especially careful, in bringing up their oldest child, to stress the value of relaxation and relationships and to lighten the emphasis on achievement.

Since later-born parents usually have a relatively relaxed attitude about achievement and place a high value on personal relationships, their first child is likely to be more relaxed and outgoing than an oldest child with first-born parents. Nevertheless, he will probably be the most achievement-oriented child in that particular family.

The Pseudo-Eldest

As Rudolf Dreikurs points out, "A child . . . born after the death of the first child . . . has a double hazard to face. He is in reality a second child living with a ghost ahead of him. At the same time he now has the position of a first child."[6]

As he grows older, this pseudo-eldest child may consciously or subconsciously wonder whether he should try to stand in for the deceased child and assuage the parents' sense of loss. Children born in this position often try to fulfill their parents' fantasies about the phantom first child.

If the first child was of the opposite sex, the second may try to compensate the parents for their loss by assuming some of the characteristics of that child's sex. I witnessed an excellent example of this type of "overcompensation" in Amon, the young woman from Thailand whom I mentioned in chapter two. When I first knew her, she constantly boasted about her strength and disdained feminine clothing and makeup. Her motto seemed to be, "Anything a man can do, I can do better." This attitude, I thought, came from being the first of a large family and, after her father's death, having to assume much of the responsibility for her mother and younger siblings.

One night, after I had finished teaching on the first child, she came up to talk to me. "You know how I always made you believe I was the first child?" she said in an embarrassed voice. "Well, it's not true. I had an older brother who died when I was a very little child."

She went on to explain that her brother had died suddenly at the age of three. Her parents never recovered from the loss and constantly reminded Amon of her inferior status—both as a girl and as the second child. Amon tried to be all her brother would have been and more. She spent almost every minute of her waking time working and caring for her family. She couldn't even admit to her closest Christian friends that she was not the first child. She had, in fact, totally repressed the memory of her brother and had become, in her mind, her parents' true first child.

The confession she made to me that night seemed to set her free from the pressure of proving herself the equal of her parents' idealized concept of her dead brother. No longer does she try to demonstrate her superiority to men. Even her physical appearance has changed: She dresses in a much more feminine way and even uses some makeup.

In cases where the second sibling is of the same sex as the one who dies, he (or she) faces another problem: that of feeling his role in life is to play the part of the deceased sibling. Pat was only two when her eight-year-old sister, Danielle, died. Danielle had been weak and crippled from birth but a beautiful child and the father's favorite. After her death, the family made frequent Sunday visits to the cemetery. Pat remembers the guilty feeling she had as they would get back in the car to leave, her parents' solemn faces a reminder of their loss and her failure to make them happy. Her parents were both alcoholics and this further convinced Pat that she had failed to make up to them for her sister's death. Pat grew up feeling guilty for being normal when Danielle had suffered so in her short life. Eventually Pat became "crippled" by fear and was housebound as an agoraphobic. Since her crippled sister's life had been cut short, Pat would be her "crippled" replacement.

To counter such competitiveness and role replacement, parents should of course tell their younger children about the deceased brother or sister, but they should do it in such a way that the burden of that life is not laid on any succeeding child. For this reason, if for no other, it is essential for parents to deal with their grief at a deep level and totally release their child to a loving, sovereign God. If they persist in holding on to their dreams for the deceased firstborn, they may easily destroy the second child's life as well.

Another type of pseudo-eldest child is the one who is the first of his sex. In some families the first boy, no matter how many older sisters he has, is treated as a first child. This is a difficult position for an easygoing later-born to assume. If he is to fill the role assigned to him, he will always have to deny his inner impulses.

The mother who has a preference for boys may excuse her first son (or sons) from responsibility for household tasks and caring for the younger children, and assign these duties to a later-born daughter, who thus becomes a pseudo-eldest child. In a study of 1,000 teenaged children, the researchers found that first-born girls did sixty percent more work than first-born boys. Later-borns were much more willing to help around the house but younger daughters still did thirty percent more work than younger boys.[7]

This heavy burden of responsibility also affects the first-born's spiritual life. If everything depends on him and his efforts, then how can he accept salvation as a gift? Even when he does come to the point of receiving Jesus as his Savior, such a child frequently falls back into the pattern of thinking, *Now it's up to me to keep my salvation.* In his search for guidelines that will ensure success, he often comes under bondage to legalism. Karl Olsson, himself a first child, calls this legalistic attitude "confidence in the flesh" (see Philippians 3:4). "Such confidence is a leading from strength. It means relating to people in terms of my performance rather than my humanity and weakness."[8]

Parents need to stress the grace aspect of Christianity especially with their first children. Studying the epistle to the Galatians would help your oldest to see that not only are we saved by grace, but we have to continue walking in grace and freedom, not performance and bondage. I find it amusing that oldest children, who tend to be legalists, usually marry youngest children, who are anything but. In fact, youngest children don't usually want to consider their responsibilities before God, but consider only the grace aspects of the Gospel. If their marriage is successful, they will be a great balance to one another.

The responsible child is often imbued with the belief that performance, rather than relationships, is what counts. The high goals we set for our first children may cause them to become perfectionists. It is not surprising that such children, according to Dr. Ross Campbell, tend toward depression as they get older. If the meaning of life lies in the achievement of goals, what happens when those goals are reached? Worse, what happens if the child fails in his attempts to reach those goals? Dr. Campbell's advice to parents is especially valuable in dealing with first-borns: "If your older adolescent has these [perfectionistic] traits, you can be of tremendous help to him by teaching him to find significance in pleasant hobbies and other means of relaxation, and especially to learn the immense value of friends and personal relationships."[9]

What Can Parents Do?

After reading about all these parent-created problems of the responsible child, you are probably wondering how you should handle your first-born—how you can prevent such difficulties, or how you can rectify the mistakes you have already made. Should we not give the eldest child any responsibility? A first-born parent who feels that his own problems are related to too much responsibility in childhood may demand too little of his own first-born, in an effort to save him from similar problems.

Edith Neisser, feels that the first-born should be given some responsibility for the younger siblings. In her book *The Eldest Child*, she says that such responsibilities, if "judiciously assigned and not overwhelming, . . . provide a way of expressing and strengthening the kindlier feelings of the first boy or girl in the family toward later arrivals."[10] Denial of responsibility for younger children may actually deprive the oldest child of an opportunity to develop desirable traits of affection and loyalty in his relationships with others.

In discussing this matter with oldest children, I have found that their resentment was not so much due to the responsibilities they were given as to the lack of privileges which, they felt, should have accompanied their greater share of responsibility.

One thirteen-year-old girl mentioned that her bedtime was only fifteen minutes later than that of her two younger siblings. "Not only that," she said in an indignant tone, "but they lie in their beds and watch the clock. If I am one minute late getting to bed, they come in and tell my mother."

Apparently first-borns wouldn't have minded being given greater responsibility as children if they had felt the rewards were sufficient. It seems important for parents to give their eldest children some special privileges in exchange for their baby-sitting and housekeeping services. The greatest desire of the oldest child seems to be a later bedtime, which emphasizes his position as the surrogate parent.

It is also important for parents to give their oldest children some time to themselves when they are protected from the intrusion of younger brothers and sisters. First-borns should have opportunities to participate in activities unrelated to the other children in the family, and should be allowed to play undisturbed when a friend comes to visit. The mother who continually tells her first-born, "Oh, let your sister play with you. Don't be so selfish," is in reality being selfish herself and failing in her responsibility of supervising the younger children.

The oldest child who is consistently expected to entertain his younger siblings may come to the point that he or she is unable to play with others without being the boss or the little mother. They need time for peer group activities, where they can learn to cooperate as well as to lead.

If you are wondering whether your oldest child is overloaded with responsibility, ask yourself these questions: Does he have time for activities with his own friends? Is he reasonably cooperative in carrying out his assigned chores? Does he get along with his peers, and is he generally well-adjusted? If you can honestly give an affirmative answer to all these questions, then you are probably not erring on the side of assigning him too much responsibility.

If the answer is no, then you need to reassess your expectations of your child and the amount of responsibility you have placed on him. Mothers who are younger children themselves often lean on a first-born child the way they leaned on older brothers and sisters, expecting them to take on part of their responsibility. If you have done that with your oldest, you need to ask his forgiveness and take immediate steps to correct the situation.

Sometimes oldest children resent their position in the family constellation because of the demands they feel are on their performance. You could help your oldest child accept his position as oldest and the accompanying responsibility by showing him the first child from God's point of view. Read with him: Exodus 13:2; Numbers 3:13; Numbers 8:17; and Luke 2:23, which says, "Every first-born male that opens the womb shall be called holy to the Lord" (NAS). That child's position as first in the family was God's choice, not yours—and in the Old Testament Jewish family God Himself assigned to the oldest son greater responsibility and corresponding privileges. The first child's inborn need to be a leader within the family should be met by the judicious assignment of special position and responsibility. In this way, parents can help their first child find fulfillment in living out God's design for his life.

We have discussed in this chapter the first-borns who take their responsibilities seriously—even too seriously. But what happens when a first-born is unable to accept responsibility? Some eldest children appear as lazy or almost nonfunctioning adults. What conditions may cause them to reject their assigned role in life? In the next chapter, we will try to answer these questions and will examine other needs of the first child.

Parenting Pointers

1. First-born parents need to be especially careful to lighten the emphasis on achievement with their own first child.

2. Parents should stress the value of hobbies and relationships and give them the same importance as achievement.

3. Parents who have a deceased child should be careful not to hold that child up as an example for later children. Their acceptance of the death will free their other children to lead their own lives.

4. Teach your child Scripture on the grace of God. Stress the continuing walking in grace of the Christian life rather than performance.

5. Make sure your oldest child has special privileges as well as responsibility. One way of making him feel special is by a later bedtime.

6. Allow your first-born to play without intrusion of younger brothers and sisters.

7. Strive for that balance between enough responsibility so your oldest's need to be a leader is fulfilled and too much responsibility which will bring discouragement.

8. Help your child to understand that God has given special honor as well as special responsibility to the first-born in Scripture.

Five

The Unachieving First-Born

The first child holds a unique position in life: He is for a period of time his parents' one and only, the sole recipient of their love and concern. He comes to believe that all life revolves around his needs and desires; he is a monarch in the domestic kingdom. Then, just as he comes to expect such royal treatment, his reign comes to an end. The second child is born. This displacement of position was called by Alfred Adler "dethronement." The only child is never dethroned, while later children have never had their parents' undivided love and attention.

Adler believes that it is this early dethronement that may determine the first child's future ability to achieve. Amazingly, if the first child takes his dethronement too seriously, he may become discouraged and lose all self-reliant powers, with the result that he will not want to accept responsibility.[1]

Dethronement

From an adult perspective it is hard to imagine what our first child experiences as he sees the new baby enter the realm he once ruled sovereignly. Edith Neisser helped me to understand the emotional turmoil of the oldest in her analogy:

> The feelings of the first-born confronted with the fact that another baby is coming have often been compared to the feelings a wife would have if her husband told her, "I love you so much I think it would be twice as nice to have two wives." Both situations entail the indignity and discomfort of having only a half interest in the person who is vital to your well being. Both would raise the question, "What is wrong with me that I am not sufficient?" "What have I done to deserve this?"[2]

The sex of the second child does nothing to alleviate the first child's anxiety and concern—either way there will be questions. If the new baby is the same sex as the first child, the question would be, "If I was an adequate boy (girl), then why did they have to go and have a second one?" If the baby is the opposite sex, the question becomes, "Wasn't I good enough? Why did they have to go and have one of those?"[3] Whatever sex, it's a no win proposition for the parents.

The age differences between the siblings will also have an effect on the conflict between the two. "When the youngest sibling is born only one or two years after the oldest, the latter sees his sibling as a rival for the care, attention, and affection of his parents as well as for their free gifts and favors, even for food."[4] At this age, the sex of the second child is not noticed; he is merely a rival for Mother's attention. The oldest may see the baby as an interesting novelty for the first few days. When he realizes the baby is "here to stay" he may begin to fight for Mother's attention.

When my friend Roz brought her new baby girl home from the hospital, her son, Nathan, was seventeen months old. "At first," she said, "he merely stared at the baby as if she were an unwelcome visitor who would soon leave." After several days, Nathan began to realize his competition was a permanent part of the domain and became very agitated when Roz picked up the baby to nurse her. At these times he would try to push the baby out of the way and climb up on her lap. Roz handled the situation wisely. She made it very clear to Nathan that he could not harm the baby but allowed him to sit next to her while she nursed and they used that opportunity to read his books together.

I also took advantage of feeding time as a way of focusing special attention on my oldest. As a result, John was not threatened by his little sister's demands to be fed but rather saw it as a time for special attention from me. When Tom was born, I continued this ritual, with John and Shannon on either side of me. Eventually reading became one of the children's favorite activities and undoubtedly contributed to their achievement in school.

If the difference in age is three to four years, "the older of two siblings feels threatened in his power and control over his parents. Greed for food and the need for affection and help are less important now. The older sibling is irked by the fact that the parents set up tasks for him (or her), but not for the younger one. He must offer returns for parental favors, whereas the younger one gets them for free."[5]

A child at age three or four may revert to babyish behavior to recapture the mother's attention. After all, if the baby is getting her attention for soiling his pants and screaming for a bottle, why shouldn't he? The wise mother will give her oldest the attention he is demanding while reassuring him that he is more grown up than the baby and is able to do many more things.

While my daughter and I were having lunch in one of the local fast food restaurants recently, our attention was drawn to a family across the aisle. The second child, a little girl about eighteen months old, kept climbing down from the booth and running around the restaurant. The father, who appeared to be a patient man, would go after her and laugh at her antics. Every so often, the older girl, about four, would try to mimic the baby—obviously to get her dad to chuckle at her, too. In response to her behavior the dad would reply: "Go sit back in the booth, you're a big girl." The little girl would climb back into the booth and continue to watch her dad so obviously enjoying her younger sister. Eventually, it would be too much for her, so she would get down, go after her sister and, of course, be sent back to the booth with a reprimand.

If only her father could have handled the situation differently. He might have said, "I'm so glad I have a big girl that I don't have to chase all around the restaurant. I'm happy you can sit and eat with Mom and me." He might have even reinforced that by giving her the special privilege of going out to eat alone with him. In this way she would see the obvious benefits of being the "big girl." When we left the restaurant, she was still sitting in the booth, longingly watching her dad following little sister around the restaurant.

If the siblings are four or five years apart, the sex of the second child is more pertinent. "The family situation can improve or worsen depending on the sex of the second-born. The child's family changes to either one with three persons of one sex and one person of the other, whose attention and affection will be sought even more vehemently, or to a family of two persons of one sex and two persons of the other sex. The latter case may smooth things out."[6]

If the age difference is six or more years, they grow up as quasi only children. The older child has established his territory and already moved out of the house for a period of time into school and activities. The only resentment this child may feel is if the parents demand too much of him in the way of responsibility and care of the new infant.

Since dethronement can be such a traumatic event in the life of a first child, we need to learn ways to soften the blow by preparing the first-born for the birth of the second. Roz mentioned that she set up the crib and changing table about a month ahead of time since the baby would have to share Nathan's room. In this way she hoped Nathan would get accustomed to this intrusion into his domain. Any changes in the child's routine should be done fairly early in the pregnancy so the child won't feel the baby has displaced it.

Joan Solomon Weiss, author of *Your Second Child*, feels many parents try to give the first child too much unnecessary information.[7] She says that many parents tell their child, "We'll love you and the baby just as much." In that way they are already setting the child up for comparison and sibling rivalry.

"You're going to love the new baby" is another common refrain of expectant parents that doesn't work. Usually, the first child feels dislike for the new baby in the beginning. She also warns against giving the child special treats during the pregnancy saying that these are "guilt-laden messages" telling the child something awful is about to happen.

Children can be prepared quite far in advance for the new baby in subtle, little ways. If you have the opportuity to visit a mother and her new baby, it would afford a wonderful opportunity to explain to your child what will be involved in caring for the new baby. Also, many young children look forward to the birth expecting an instant playmate. This would be a good opportunity to dispel any such notion in your first child and help avoid future disappointment.

Mom and Dad can take turns bathing the child, preparing meals, and reading the bedtime story. In this way the child won't be devastated when his mother leaves for the hospital. It would be a good idea to have your child well acquainted with the person he will be staying with while Mom is in the hospital. If he will also be staying away from home, a few overnights before the baby is born might be advisable.

Even young children can be told about the new baby, allowed to feel it kicking in Mom's stomach and even read library books on the subject in the child's age category. Beware of too much preparation, though. Although the pregnancy is a major part of the mother's life, it is a very small part of your child's and too much focus on the "new baby" may cause the child undue concern and anxiety.

No matter how careful we are in preparing the first-borns, we cannot save them from some anxiety and jealousy toward the new baby. After all, it does mean a shift in roles and less time and attention for the first child. It will be some time before the oldest sees that the baby can bring fun and companionship. We can, however, help ease them through this difficult time.

Often, the first child reacts by fighting for his mother's love. "If the mother fights back at him, the child will become high-tempered, wild, critical, and disobedient."[8] The mother "fights back" at her child by responding to his behavioral changes (bed-wetting, hostility to the baby, disobedience, etc.) with a show of power. She may try to force him by threats and discipline back into the good little child he was before the baby. Parents, and especially Mother, need to be aware of the heightened sensitivity and hostility that the first child may experience. If she realizes that this "monster," who was once her adored, well-behaved first child, will soon adjust to sharing her attention, she can react with less fear to his displays of anger. If she continues to fight her first child, she may set up a situation that will continue throughout the life of that oldest.

In fact, open resentment on the part of the first-born may be more acceptable than repressed anger. Edith Neisser says that "preoccupation with the baby, fear lest some harm might come to it, insistence on staying near it are usually only a disguise, and a thin one at that, for a strong desire to have the rival out of the way."[9] She goes on to say that this might continue in later life in a domination of the mother who could not be possessed in childhood and a compulsion to manage the affairs of others. While convincing himself that he (or she) is self-sacrificing, he is really punishing others.

There is bound to be some jealousy and some behavioral

changes in your first child with the birth of the second. These changes may not show up until after the novelty of the new baby has worn off, and your first-born realizes the full impact of his displacement. Children are different in their responses: one may show his displeasure through bed-wetting or withdrawal, another by trying to hurt the baby, and still another by an oversolicitous attitude. The mother should respond with understanding, over-looking some of the lapses in toilet training or other recurrences of infantile behavior. She cannot allow anything that would harm the baby but she can react with firmness rather than anger. At these times it might be helpful if Mother could say to her child: "I know you are feeling angry at me and the baby right now because you feel I don't care about you anymore." Then she could go on to reassure her child that her feelings toward him have not changed. The child is only acting up because he feels he has lost his mother's love so, if she reacts in a negative, angry way toward him, she will just reinforce this belief. If, instead, Mother uses this as an opportunity to reassure him, his fear will be laid to rest and he won't have to fight to get her attention. Usually most of these reactions will disappear within a few months as the new baby becomes an integral part of the household routine.

Dethronement Later in Life

We generally think of dethronement occurring when the sec-ond child is born. Actually, dethronement can occur anytime in the life of the first child, if he feels the second has taken his place in the family. In the Bible, Jacob, the second-born, stole the birthright from his first-born brother, Esau, when they were adults (Genesis 27). Chuck, a thirty-five-year-old man in our fellow-ship, recounted a similar story.

Chuck and his wife, Roz, were in our Sunday night house church meeting of twelve adults. Roz was sharing the fear and insecurity she was experiencing because Chuck had been out of work for two months. Chuck is a college-educated man and also a talented musician but he had been unable to find a job.

"The real problem," Roz said softly, "is his lack of ambition and apparent unconcern about the situation. That's what really has me worried."

We began to question Chuck about his background. He was the oldest of three children but he certainly did not fit the usual first-born pattern of responsible, conservative achiever.

"I think my life followed a pretty normal pattern of development in my early years," he said. "I was a 'typical' first child—obedient, good in school, and I was even an Eagle Scout."

Chuck went on to tell us that during his last two years of high school he got involved with a rock band. Music took first place in his life and his studies fell off. Because of this, he flunked two subjects his senior year and was not allowed to graduate with his class. He was deeply humiliated and felt he had let his parents down. He did make up the two classes in summer school but his dad didn't even come to his graduation.

For about five years he traveled with a rock band and was heavily involved in drugs and alcohol. After he had given Jesus Christ control of his life, he went to college. Still, something was missing in his life—that intangible element of confidence and assurance. Instead, Chuck seemed almost resigned to the fact that he would always be a failure.

Trying to find direction for his life, he joined the Navy and finally began to assume leadership positions and develop the self-confidence he had lost. He left the Navy with an optimistic outlook but when he returned home he found that his second-born brother (three years younger) had supplanted him in the eyes of the family. He had stolen his birthright!

"He became everything I wasn't to my parents. He even treated me as the younger brother—yelling at me for my behavior. I felt I had failed my parents and could never again win first place in their hearts. It was downhill from then on."

As Chuck came to the conclusion of his story, each of us could understand the reason behind his defeatist attitude. After you have lost the number one spot, what's left? Also, just as Chuck felt he had disappointed his parents, now he was disappointing his wife.

My husband explained to Chuck that not only did he have to forgive his parents, he also had to forgive himself. After a tearful session of forgiveness, we suggested that he pray about it with his parents, who were committed Christians, and settle it once and for all.

The next week, after praying with his parents, he had several job interviews and reported a confidence he had not felt in years. He knew he made a good impression on the interviews and reported happily that he was offered a job at the firm he preferred. After two years, he is progressing well in his company and has remained confident in his ability to succeed.

Some time after our night in house church with Chuck, his parents both died suddenly within several months of each other. God's timing is so perfect. Chuck would never have been able to pray with them and get that release if he had waited even six months. As it worked out, God brought a wonderful healing in their relationship and they were able to spend those last months together in a new understanding and fellowship. Although their deaths were sudden and unexpected, Chuck had a beautiful peace in his heart that all hurtful issues between them had been settled. Because of this, he could accept their deaths without anger or excessive grief.

Chuck was dethroned suddenly when he returned from the Navy, but dethronement can also be a gradual process. It often happens that the second child is quicker and sharper than the first, especially if the first is a boy and the second a girl. Girls develop more quickly, bodily and mentally, than boys till about their sixteenth year and a second-born sister might overtake her older brother. Rudolf Dreikurs feels that the "knowledge that a first child is discouraged by the rapid advancement of the second child permits the parents to give added encouragement to him so that he gains confidence in his own abilities."[10]

If your second child is achieving and competitive, and your first is quiet and an underachiever, the first is probably a discouraged first-born who feels he has already lost the race. The parents need to find ways to restore his leadership to him. Discover his talents and interests. Most schools today offer testing services to parents or could at least recommend where to find them. These tests would pinpoint those areas where the first child would be successful. Also, take into consideration interests that may be dormant in your first child. Perhaps he has always wanted to take a computer course, or a painting class. Encourage him in these areas. It is important that parents recognize this situation before the habit of discouragement has become settled in the mind of your child. Otherwise, parents can subtly give away their first child's birthright to the perceptive second child.

This seemed to be the situation with a friend of mine who came to see me about her oldest child, a son Tom. He was not following the usual oldest-child role of responsible development but was, in her words, "flaky and irresponsible."

As we talked I discovered that because of Tom's irresponsible attitude she was giving the second boy the responsibilities usually meted out to the oldest. If the children went to the movies, younger brother would carry the money because "spacey Tom might lose it." If the ice cream truck came down the block, younger brother would be the one to buy the ice cream and dole it out to the rest of the children.

Little by little my friend was usurping Tom's role of ruler over his sibling subjects. In doing this, she was reinforcing Tom's tendency toward carelessness, and lowering his self-esteem. She decided to restore to Tom the rights and privileges of eldest. The next Saturday, with much prayer and trepidation, she sent the children off to the movies with Tom in charge of the money. To her amazement, Tom took his new responsibility seriously and has done a real turnaround in his behavior. His mother's trust brought responsibility, which in turn taught him to discipline his mind and pay attention to what was going on around him. This inner discipline brought an improvement in grades, which in turn engendered a better self-image.

There are two other reasons first children may not achieve at levels they are capable of. One is parental preference of a later-born. The other is expecting too much from that willing-to-please oldest child.

Parental Preference

Sometimes first children do not succeed simply because the mother prefers the second child. Perhaps he (or she) is more sensitive and introverted and this personality type blends better with the female temperament. We see this illustrated with Rebekah's two sons, Esau and Jacob. Esau was "a skillful hunter, a man of the field; but Jacob was a peaceful man, living in tents" (Genesis 25:27, NAS).

Isaac preferred Esau who had an aggressive, outgoing nature while "Rebekah loved Jacob." She wanted her favorite second son to be the inheritor of the birthright and so she cunningly arranged to deprive her first child of that right. In like manner, mothers, for one reason or another, may subconsciously want to dethrone their first child and give his title to the second. Mothers must realize the effect their powerful influence has on all their children and not favor one child at the expense of another.

In the case of shotgun or pressured marriages both parents may reject the first-born. The first child is a continual reminder of the parents' sin, so often he or she is ignored or becomes the target for her parents' anger and resentment. One mother constantly told her first-born daughter, "If it weren't for you, we wouldn't be married." Because the marriage was bad, the daughter blamed herself for her parents' unhappiness. "If only I hadn't been born," she said continually, until the day she decided to release every-one from the unhappy situation by committing suicide. In this type of marriage, the second child will not bear the stigma of shame so will usually become like a first and the inheritor of the birthright.

These first children, who have continually felt pushed aside and have failed to win their parents' love and approval, will usually be loners throughout life. When these youngsters start school, they will see the other children as a multiplication of the brothers and sisters they left at home. This is another situation in which he must vie for the favor of the authority figure or teacher. Since he was unsuccessful at home in winning a place in the family, he reasons subconsciously, he will probably be unsuccessful in school. So begins a process of dropping out of life and any competitive situation.

If you had to get married because of pregnancy, then your first child may carry a curse of rejection and shame from the womb. No matter how much you love and encourage your child, this early bondage may prevent him from ever being successful in life. You need to pray and ask God's forgiveness, first, for your sin of fornication (1 Corinthians 6:18), and then for any feelings of anger and hostility toward this child conceived out of wedlock. After this, accept your first child as God's gift (not punishment for your sin) and release him back to God.

Too High Expectations

The second reason first children may underachieve, besides parental preference of a later-born, is the enormous pressure for achievement is placed on the first-born—especially on oldest boys. In the last chapter we discussed signs that parents can look for if they have overloaded their first child with responsibility. The same holds true for parental expectations. Parents have such high expectations for their oldest sibling that the child is often "beaten before he begins," and decides to abdicate his number one position. Often he passes his birthright down to the next sibling and lets him deal with the demands of parental pressure.

Bradford Wilson and George Edington, both clinical psychologists, have found that in this situation

> something seems to crack under the pressure of so many seeming demands for you to achieve perfection, and so by way of protest you may wind up being almost a caricature of failure.[11]

First Steps

What if your first-born child is well on the road to failure or, worse, what if he has already left your home and you realize now your contribution to his failure? I don't believe it is ever too late for God to change a situation. In fact, God often works most miraculously at the eleventh hour. The first step is always the same: repentance. We need to confess our failure before God and in so doing "loose" the bondage (Matthew 18:18) we have put on our child by our lack of acceptance, excessive anger, failure to understand, or poor parenting.

After repentance we can then pray to accept our son or daughter exactly as God made him or her. Of course, we can continue to pray that God will make up for our mistakes—something He is very good at doing—and in that way get the glory.

Then we can dedicate our oldest to the Lord. There is something mystical about that first child. In the Old Testament, God required that the parents dedicate their first-born son to the Lord (Exodus 13:2,12; Numbers 3:13; 8:17). We parents seldom have a relationship with a later child that is as intense and close as our relationship with our first-born. We invest so much in that first child—all our hopes, our unfulfilled dreams, our weaknesses, and even our hurts: They are all going to be healed by the life of that first child. On their shoulders is the burden to either prove or deny our value as persons. All our credibility as parents is resting on them.

Because of this emotional investment and their power over our self-image, if they do not follow the plan we have chosen for them (perhaps subconsciously) we are tremendously disappointed in them. Maybe we don't say it and even think we are hiding it as we tell them: "Well, you have to do what you want." They know. They have disappointed the two people whose approval they need more than anything else in the world and this realization may doom them to failure the rest of their lives.

It is interesting that the only children God tells us to dedicate to Him are our first children. Could it be because He knows all our secret ambitions are tied up in this child? That when we dedicate this child we are also putting *our* future into His hands?

Christian parents should, of course, dedicate each of their children to the Lord, but especially their first child. He or she most represents our future and, as we give that child to God, we are saying: "We trust You, God, with our future; have *Your* way." The first child will then be released to follow God's pattern for his life rather than a rerun of our own desires.

If your child is still at home, he needs your approval desperately. Approval is the "stuff" that changes a discouraged, listless first-born into a motivated achiever. In the next chapter we will conclude our look at the first-born with the reasons approval is so important, and we will find specific ways of transforming that oldest child into the responsible, reliable, not overburdened person that God created him or her to be.

Parenting Pointers

1. Start preparing your first child far in advance for the birth of the baby by visiting a new baby, reading books, letting Dad have a part in feeding and bathing the child, and spending some time with the person who will stay with him while Mom is in the hospital.

2. Do not overprepare the child by anticipating questions he would not think to ask or trying to explain changes in the routine that will occur. Let questions and discussions develop naturally.

3. Parents should be prepared for some changes in their first-

born when the new baby comes home. Mother will need to be patient and overlook some regressions in behavior. She should not "fight back" with excessive anger or discipline.

4. Use the new baby's feeding time as a way of focusing special attention on the older child (or children) by reading or talking.

5. Be careful that the second child does not supplant the first-born. Make sure your first child has specific areas of leadership and, if he tends to be discouraged, look for areas of special interest to stimulate him.

6. In the case of a "shotgun" marriage, parents must be careful that they do not blame the child for the problems in the marriage. You may need to pray and ask forgiveness for this attitude.

7. Be careful that you do not place your expectations on the child but allow God to direct his life.

8. Dedicate your first-born to God.

Six

The Importance
of Approval

Since the first child is the embodiment of the hopes and dreams of the parents and has the closest relationship with them, why are so many mothers and fathers in conflict with their oldest children? Parents are often frustrated by a love-hate relationship with the first child that is much more intense than with any of the later-born children.

Parents' Suppressed Guilt

The roots of this hostility reach 'way back to the days of infancy of the first child. First-time mothers (and also fathers) have a great deal of anxiety in caring for their first child. In addition to that anxiety is the ignorance and frustration of first-time parenting. Most mothers will readily agree that they learned on their oldest and the later children received the benefits.

71

I can remember vividly the frustration I felt when my first child, John, was changed, fed, and burped, but continued to cry. I was sure that, because of my inexperience, I was neglecting something vital to his well being. How many times I thought: *If he could only talk and tell me what he needs.*

Joan Lasko in her research study of parent reactions to first and second children discovered that many parents, and especially the mother, feel inadequate in handling the first child and this inadequacy leads to hostility toward the child. She found that the mother,

> . . . when she perceives herself as committing "errors" in her handling of the child, whether from inexperience or misconceptions about child development, the guilt engendered is likely to produce hostility, in its turn. With or without such hostility, however, there is the likelihood that the mother is less spontaneous and consistent in her expression of warmth to the first child than she is in her attitude toward subsequent children.[1]

Although I did have a much closer relationship with my oldest, it is true, as Dr. Lasko discovered, that I didn't enjoy him as much as my later children. Every little problem seemed such a major obstacle and Dr. Spock was my daily "bible." I was constantly worried that I would make the wrong decision, so I read and reread and called my pediatrician so often that the nurse knew me by my worried hello. By the time I had my second child, Dr. Spock was on the shelf since I trusted more in my ability as a mother and my grateful pediatrician stopped receiving his daily, frantic phone calls.

John and I had a good relationship until his junior year of high school—then it deteriorated rapidly. We couldn't even be in the same room without getting into an argument. I was shocked by the hostility I felt toward him at times; I couldn't understand what was happening. I began to pray daily that God would reveal the source of the conflict within me so that I could be set free.

One day while praying, I began to remember those first few months after I brought John home from the hospital. I had been a career girl with little interest in marriage and motherhood. I didn't baby-sit as a young girl and had never even changed a diaper or given a baby a bottle. Now, here I was, with a child of my own. I remembered those first few nights home from the hospital, lying in bed tense, unable to sleep, waiting for John's cry. The minute he uttered his first whimper, I was up and ready to feed him. I became his slave, and began to resent this minute master who had invaded my life and destroyed my self-esteem. I'm sure that my directing all my tension toward him was the main reason John developed colic. Eventually, he even had to have sedative drops before his feedings so he could retain his food. Then I began to have severe attacks of chest pain that were eventually diagnosed as gall bladder problems and required surgery. I believe both conditions were the result of the severe stress I felt at that time.

Although I loved my first child deeply, I also felt woefully inadequate as a mother. Who was making me feel this way? John, of course. These ambivalent feelings were the beginning of my love-hate relationship with him. Years later I realized that the hostility I was feeling toward the teenage John, who was going through the normal adolescent problems of moodiness and rebellion, was simply a replay of the hostility I felt toward him as a little baby. Once again he was at a stage of life for which I had no preparation and my inability to understand him just added to the anxiety.

When I realized the root of my hostility, I began to pray to forgive John for making me feel so inadequate. I pictured myself as that frustrated young mother and asked God's forgiveness for my inability to cope with and accept the situation. I also forgave John and released him from the resentment I felt toward him. There was an immediate change in our relationship.

Since John was the first of my children to initiate me into the wonderful and bewildering world of teens, I still reacted occasionally to situations that I would come to accept as normal in my later children, but I never again felt that overwhelming hostility toward John. Once he left for college and was released from his home environment, our relationship was totally healed.

The First-Born's Sense of Guilt

Just as the parents have the deepest sense of guilt toward their first child, so the first child also has the strictest conscience and is the most prone to a guilt complex. The roots of the first child's guilt, like the parents', are buried in his early childhood.

Guilt Toward Siblings

As I mentioned in the last chapter, the first-born often experiences hostility and jealousy toward the new baby. He cannot justify his resentment, however, because he knows that little babies are entitled to extra attention from the mother. As a result, he has a predisposition to guilt because of his negative feelings toward the younger child.

Later-born children have no such guilt complex. They can easily justify their anger and resentment toward older siblings because they are usually domineering and bossy. In addition, the eldest usually enjoys privileges that the younger child does not and this too engenders resentment from the younger child.

Self-Disapproval

In addition to this guilt over the later-born child, there are several other situations that predispose the first child to a guilt complex. One is a tendency to be severely self-critical.

Once when John was struggling through a difficult university curriculum, he was upset one marking period because he didn't receive an A in two classes. I tried to assure him that his father and I were proud of him and it didn't matter to us if he didn't get all A's.

"I know," was his immediate reply, "but it matters to me." After all those years of imposing our standards upon him, John had now incorporated those standards and carried his "parent" within him. Because of this self-critical perfectionism, first children often turn their hostile and aggressive emotions inward and struggle with depression.

The personality disorder that is called obsessive-compulsive is usually related to excessive development of the conscience. In a 1967 study of the obsessive-compulsive character, an overwhelmingly large proportion of a group of patients under observation were found to be first-born.[2]

Taking Another Role

Another reason first children develop a burdensome conscience is that, with their responsible natures, they may try to be adult beyond their years. I mentioned in chapter four that this high sense of responsibility will tend to make them feel accountable for many things that happen around them. Even with their many achievements there is always an undertone of guilt. Karl König, the German psychiatrist, feels this is

. . . because they had to forgo certain possibilities open to others since their early childhood. The first child has to defend even when he would like to attack; he has to comply even when he thought it wrong to do so. The first child will often obey when he would like to revolt.[3]

In other words, first children are almost always acting in opposition to their true feelings. This inner knowledge leaves them feeling guilty and hypercritical. Unfortunately, it may become a life pattern.

Parents have to be especially careful with their first child that they do not play on their sensitive consciences to force the child into acceptable behavior. Mothers need to be especially careful not to use manipulative statements such as: "If you really loved me you would————"; "Don't make that noise because you give me a headache when you do that"; "Mommy doesn't feel good today so please be a good boy"; or "If you eat all your vegetables you will make me so happy." Instead, we need to convey to the child that even though he misbehaves, we will still love him. Parents should also avoid too much exhortation about being a good boy or girl, especially when the second child arrives.

If I could do anything different in raising my children, I would be less cautious and overprotective—especially with John. At Christmastime last year, John came in the house covered with mud from head to toe. He had been playing touch football with a group of his friends, also home on vacation.

"Why," I said, staring disapprovingly, "would a twenty-three-year-old man want to go out and play in the mud?"

Without so much as a pause, he replied: "Because my mother never let me get dirty when I was little."

I had no answer; it was absolutely true.

As a result of the guilt and tension between first children and their parents and also the restrictiveness with which parents raise their oldest, it is not surprising that first children have more anxiety than later-borns. The first-born will usually be the prime worrier in the family, which adds to his serious approach to life.

In experiments at the University of Nebraska, researchers found that in anxiety-arousing situations, first-borns tend to seek the company of others much more than later-borns do.[4] They said this was like a child in stress seeking his parents.

When John had a difficult time academically his first year of college, we finally realized this was due not to basic intelligence (he won a state scholarship) but to the size of the school. On that campus of about 35,000 students, he could not find a parent figure to relate to. The professors lectured to groups of hundreds and in the more intimate setting of the labs, there was a student leader. Because of this, he called home quite frequently just to talk and calm his anxiety in the new surroundings. First children would probably do better in smaller schools with closer relationships of teachers and students.

First children, to function at their fullest potential, need to be able to relate closely to an authority figure. This relationship seems to provide the reassurance and approval they need to allay the anxiety in new situations.

The Need for Approval

First children because of their sensitive consciences and tendency toward guilt and anxiety have the deepest need of approval of any of the children in the family constellation. Because of this intense desire for approval, the first child may be exploited by domineering parents.

I have already mentioned that first children receive the full brunt of parental authority and expectations. They also receive the strictest discipline. Actually, first children, because of their sensitivity and desire to please their parents, should be the easiest to discipline. The first child who has been handled correctly by his parents will respond better to psychological discipline rather than physical punishment. Verbal rebukes and visual disapproval are often enough to correct the oldest. Since the first child desires the parents' approval, withholding that approval may be the best form of discipline.

Domineering parental authority will stifle individuality and self-expression. If a child is not allowed to be himself, he can never mature. The mother who brags about her "perfect little child who never gives her a bit of trouble" may be raising a robot who is giving her exactly what she wants but not learning to be himself.

Mary was a model child and appeared to be a perfect little Christian. She was the eldest of five children and her parents' pride and joy. When it was time to go to college, she chose, of course, a wonderful Christian school. During her third year she had to transfer to a state school because she needed some courses for her major that were not offered at the Christian school. At the state school, she decided to change her major to Theatre. Her parents strongly objected to this change, arguing that "theatre people" were very worldly and they didn't want her around them. Mary was twenty-one and had always obeyed her parents' wishes but this time she stood firm.

Their response was to insist adamantly that she stay with her original major or they would not continue to pay for her education. Mary was forced into a no-win decision by her parents: She could do what she had always done—give in and continue to let them live her life—or she could rebel. She chose to rebel. She also decided to go a step further in her rebellion and moved in with her boyfriend.

Mary's parents could have used this situation to release their approval-seeking first child and demonstrate to her that their love, like God's, was not dependent on her outward conformity. They could have said: "Mary, you know we are not in favor of your change of curriculum, but we believe you are a responsible girl who is committed to Jesus. We will support you in this change. If you decide later that it was a mistake, don't worry, you can always go back to your original major." That's all Mary was looking for—a chance to make her own decisions about her life instead of always being forced to live out her parents' wishes. Instead, Mary's parents pushed her over the edge and into a rebellious pattern of behavior.

Parental domination may produce children who are outwardly obedient but it predisposes them to other more serious problems. Edith Neisser, in *The Eldest Child*, feels that this type of domination may be at the root of many of the learning problems of the eldest child.

Happy, healthy children have a lively curiosity and usually enjoy attacking a problem. If they continually resist learning there is a deeper reason. That reason in an eldest often is that he has been so impressed with the wrongness of competing, showing off, or being curious that unconsciously he feels it is safer to retreat than to put himself forward in any way. Approval, he believes, can only come from being self-effacing, and not learning is a kind of self-effacement.[5]

As Christian parents, we want our children to develop Christlike character. But the imposition of authority cannot produce virtue. It may produce conformity in our first children because they want our approval but it will not produce character. John Powell, the popular psychologist, says that in studying human motivation

positive reinforcements of the will (reward for good conduct) are infinitely more effective than negative reinforcements (punishments for bad conduct). To be constantly critical of a young person is obviously a dangerous thing. It tends to undermine his confidence and to make all authority obnoxious. However, if one takes the approach of positive reinforcements, tending to overlook small failures in conduct but never failing to recognize and reward (at least with a kind word) the desired conduct, the effect will be almost magical.[6]

We are quicker to criticize our first children for not meeting our high standards than we are to praise them for good conduct. It is important that their good behavior be noticed and praised or they may feel they can never please and give up even trying.

I first became aware of this deep need in my oldest during an outing at the local beach. All four children were playing in the water, attempting to swim, dive, and float. John kept calling to me to watch what he could do. Then he would keep his eyes fastened on me to see if I was watching. The other three were content to play and enjoy themselves, but even John's play needed my stamp of approval.

Esau, the first-born twin of Isaac, had several Hittite wives. Marrying against the ordinance of God did not bother Esau until he saw it was displeasing to his parents.

> Now Esau saw that Isaac had blessed Jacob and sent him away to Paddan-aram, to take to himself a wife from there, and that when he blessed him he charged him, saying, "You shall not take a wife from the daughters of Canaan." . . . So Esau saw that the daughters of Canaan displeased his father Isaac; and Esau went to Ishmael, and married, besides the wives that he had, Mahalath the daughter of Ishmael, Abraham's son. . . .
>
> Genesis 28:6–8, NAS

Esau couldn't stand to see Jacob win his father's approval and was willing to do anything to gain that approval himself.

This lines up with some experiments done with first and later children. The experiments found that "first children tended to conform more when they felt moderate acceptance from others, as if they could win more acceptance by conforming."[7] Also, they conformed more to group standards, especially when the degree of conformity was public.

Because first children will conform to be accepted, principally by parents, we have a tremendous responsibility to let them know they are loved and accepted even, or especially, when they are not doing everything we want them to do. Otherwise, a pattern of conforming will develop that may keep them from ever moving into a real relationship with God. The first child who goes through adolescent rebellion is often trying to find out if his parents will still love him even if he doesn't do everything they say. Many of his actions may be crying, "Do you love me for me?" Those times of rebellion afford us parents a chance to love our children as God loves us and help our first-born understand that God's grace is not dependent on what we do but on who we are.

When John turned eighteen, we gave him a special birthday present. We wrote him a letter reassuring him of our love and appreciation. We expressed our pride in him and the character-istics of faithfulness and loyalty that marked his life. We told him that now he was a man and needed to begin looking to his heavenly Father for approval and direction. Then we prayed for him releasing him from any bondage he had to us and to our expectations for him. Together John and I released him into God's hands and broke our control over him.

The first-born child who feels he has satisfied his parents' expectations and is totally accepted by them is then free to trans-fer the desire to please to God. Too many first children feel they have failed their parents and remain in bondage the rest of their lives, always seeking approval from authority figures and never able to relate to their heavenly Father. It might be helpful to have your first-born study the life of Jesus, a first-born Son, who al-ways did His Father's will and was not swayed even by the pres-sures of His family (Matthew 12:46–50; John 2:4; John 7:2–10). Jesus never did anything in response to pressure from people, but only when He knew it was also His Father's will. "Truly, truly, I say to you, the Son can do nothing of Himself, unless it is something He sees the Father doing; for whatever the Father does, these things the Son also does in like manner" (John 5:19, NAS). In this way you could teach your conforming, people-pleasing first child that it is only doing God the Father's will that is important.

One way to help your first child learn good behavior patterns that will gain your needed approval is to set fair but firm limits for him. Because of their sensitive consciences, they need definite guidelines to follow until they develop their own inner guide-lines. First children tend to be more legalistic and like specific rules governing things like bedtimes and caring for their rooms. Also, we need to be consistent in our punishment when they violate these guidelines.

When John was about six years old, my husband saw him throwing stones in the front yard. He went out to tell him to stop and warn him that he might break a window. John ignored the warning and, of course, broke the garage window. My husband, who at that time was not a disciplinarian, went out and scolded him for breaking the window but did not issue a punishment.

Several years after that, when John and I were praying together, he told me he still felt guilty about the broken garage window.

"Why," I asked, "would you still feel guilty? Dad didn't even spank you."

"That's the problem," said John. "I didn't get punished so I still feel guilty."

A later-born child would have felt relieved that he wasn't punished but the first child, who knows so well the consequences of his actions, needs a punishment consistent with the violation to feel relieved of his sin. A light spanking or an hour in his room would have relieved John of the guilt he felt and released his conscience.

The need for approval can be a weakness in your first child if it ties him into always seeking that approval from authority figures and conforming to their expectations. It can also be a strength. God has promised to make our weakness His strength (2 Corinthians 12:9). The wise parent will fulfill the first-born's need for approval and use it—not to manipulate, but to stimulate growth in godly character qualities by praise and encouragement. Encourage his need for approval, but teach him that true approval will only come from doing the will of God the Father.

Lucille Forer offers some encouragement to parents who may be frustrated in their relationship with the first child. She says that much of his behavior is just an attempt to adjust to sibling competition for the parents' affection and attention.

While he is adjusting to the existence of sibling rivals for the parents, he is slowly assimilating the parents' standards of what is right and wrong, of what should and should not be done. The rebelliousness that he so often exhibits during this process very often obscures the direction of his development and his parents may believe that he is well on his way to "ruin." They are, then, extremely surprised to see their child change slowly from being a rebellious, angry child or adolescent to a responsible and productive individual in later adolescence or adulthood.[8]

Spiritual Gifts

In fact, because oldest children are so often the guides and pathfinders for the rest of the kids in the family, you will find that they make excellent teachers in the Body of Christ. They are used to instructing younger brothers and sisters on the wiles and snares awaiting them in the world outside of the home that they have already conquered. Because the first-born is neither child nor parent but suspended between both worlds, he is more often a loner than later children and, for this reason, would not mind the loneliness associated with the preparation of teaching material. Also, all first-borns (including onlies) are more comfortable working with ideas rather than with people. They tend to choose professions such as mathematics, architecture, medicine, and chemistry while later children are more apt to choose service type professions relating to people.

You would think the first-born male would make a good pastor or shepherd because of his position of responsibility in his natural family. While he does grow up feeling responsible for his younger brothers and sisters, however, he does not identify with them but is rather separated from them—a leader who leads by example and teaching but not by identification and close relationships. To be successful, a good pastor should make his people feel that he truly cares about each one of them and that they have a special relationship with him. The first child always maintains that somewhat aloof position from his subjects as a way of upholding his authority. Thus, many pastors who are first-born children are gifted teachers, but unable to shepherd their people. Many first-borns do, however, make wonderful apostles, starting churches, assigning elders to care for the people, and then moving on to another location. They function well in a parental role to those churches under their care while maintaining their separateness as overseer.

Another ministry that the first-born might excel in is that of evangelist or preacher. First children (especially boys) rank higher in verbal skills than children in any other ordinal position probably because mothers spend more time talking to first children. They are usually articulate and make good salesmen. In the Church, they may function as evangelists or preachers "selling" Christianity to an unbelieving world.

So take heart. God is more than equal to the challenge. Dedicate this child to Him and love him freely "for love makes up for many of your faults" (1 Peter 4:8, LB).

Parenting Pointers

1. Recognize any hostile feelings you may have toward your first-born as a result of your inexperience as a parent. Pray and forgive him and yourself for your feelings of hostility.

2. Remember: Your first child is the most prone to a guilt complex. Do not play on his sensitive conscience or try to force him into acceptable behavior.

3. Use the opportunities of your child's rebellion to reinforce your love and acceptance of him. Let him know that, even though you do not approve of his behavior, you still love him.

4. Be liberal in your praise and encouragement.

5. Study the life of Jesus with special emphasis on His always doing the will of His Father.

6. Make sure you set fair but firm limits for him and that he is aware of the house rules and penalties.

7. Give him the freedom to break away from your domination so that he will also have the freedom to return.

Seven

Second Time Around

In spite of all the anxiety and fear about parenting a first child, we usually manage somehow and find, to our surprise, that our first-born has survived and even thrived with two inexperienced parents. When we are expecting a second child, we are therefore much less anxious and fearful about our ability to take care of a baby's physical needs. "If I did it once, I can do it again" is our new motto. In view of this, it is surprising that research shows "women having a second (or subsequent) baby have more emotional problems and are more irritable and depressed than women having a first."[1] One study even found that a full fifty percent more repeater pregnancies had emotional difficulties.

If we are more sure of our abilities, what is it about the second pregnancy that causes emotional strain? Thinking back to my own second pregnancy, I remembered the primary feeling was a fear I would not be able to love a second child as much as I loved my first. Mothers develop such an intense relationship with the first child that they worry what effect this second child will have on that relationship.

Also, Mother is so involved with the first child and his needs and demands that she can't give as much thought to the second pregnancy. This is far different from the first pregnancy when almost every waking minute was given over to wondering about the first child: What sex will it be? Will it be healthy? Will we have enough money? Can we make the transition to parenthood?

The second time around our thoughts are still focused on the first child: How will he/she accept the baby? How can I prepare my first-born for the new baby? Who will I get to stay with him when I go to the hospital? This worry about the first child and the subconscious guilt because we are not as concerned about the second child may cause some of the emotional stress that second-time mothers experience.

Surprisingly, and subsconsciously, this second child is viewed almost as an intruder into the intimate relationship we have established with our first-born. This is true even if we planned the second pregnancy. There is still that fear of the unknown. Perhaps this is why second-time mothers "are not as affectionate in the beginning."[2] Although researchers found mothers eventually become even warmer toward their second child than their first, they seem to hold back their feelings in the beginning. Perhaps they fear they will stir up the first child's jealousy toward the second or they may even resent this second child because of the problems the first child develops in response to a new baby in the home. Eventually, though, they are less likely to spank and more likely to praise their second than their first.

While the second starts off life with a less affectionate mother, there is greater consistency in the affection given. The first child, however, experiences a drastic change. He is used to an intense relationship with Mother waiting to fulfill his every need, and then, after the birth of the second, feels a sharp drop-off in the attention he gets. Two researchers, Judy Dunn and Carol Kendrick, studied 41 families from one to three months before the birth of the second child until the second child was fourteen months old.[3] They found there was a decrease in maternal playful attention toward the first child after the arrival of the second. The decrease was especially noticeable in those areas they called "sensitive attention," that is, those areas where the mother was sensitive to the child's needs and where she initiated conversations and games. After the birth of the second child, the first had to assume more responsibility for initiating both games and conversation because his mother was too preoccupied to anticipate his needs.

In some ways it's a no-win situation for Mother: She feels guilty giving too much attention to the second-born, and yet has less time to notice the unspoken needs of her first-born. "Research has shown that the stress of sibling birth is reduced if the father actively cares for the older child."[4] It is a good chance for Father to become a hero to his first-born child and form a relationship that will last a lifetime. If Father is ready to fill the gap in Mother's attention created by the arrival of the second child, many potential problems with the first will be avoided.

Because Mother is much more confident about her abilities, she does not convey her nervousness and inexperience to her baby during feeding, bathing, and changing him as she did to her first. As a result, the second child is usually more placid and relaxed than the first child. The mother takes advantage of this "good" baby to give her first child as much time and attention as she can.

My second child, Shannon, fourteen months younger than John, was not a placid child at birth. She had long periods of wakefulness during the day and would cry constantly if not held. Since I could not hold her all day long and because I was concerned about my first-born's reaction to the baby, I would sometimes let her cry in her crib while I read to John or played a game with him. In this way I was subtly telling John he was much more important than the baby and reinforcing his "kingpin" status. Also, to have a peaceful dinnertime, I would put her upstairs in her crib, close the door, and let her cry for the half-hour or forty-five minutes that we were eating. I prided myself on the fact that I was not letting a demanding baby upset our dinner. I also felt it was good for Shannon to realize she couldn't run the household.

Now researchers have found that if a crying baby is not picked up he feels that what he does doesn't matter. Later in life he may develop a "Why try?" attitude. A prompt response helps a child to develop basic trust and a strong sense of self that what he does matters in the world.[5] The times when I didn't respond to Shannon's crying, I'm sure, are partly responsible for the deep rejection and poor self-image that she had to battle later in life. It's ironic that Shannon's extreme passivity is the one thing about her I would like to change, while I am partly responsible for that attitude. Sometimes it is impossible for a busy mother of two children to attend immediately to a crying child, but we should never allow him to cry for long periods. A delayed response is still better than no response at all.

Studies show that

mothers spent significantly less time in social, affectionate, and caretaking interaction (except for feeding activities) with their second borns than they had with their firstborns; this difference was greater if the second born was female.[6]

Second-born girls suffered the greatest neglect, especially if second to a sister. The second-born boy who had an older sister was the only one who did not suffer any loss of maternal attention. Mothers are still very proud of producing a male offspring and the novelty does not seem to wear off.

Michael Lewis and Valerie S. Kreitzberg of the Educational Testing Service found that the space between children greatly influenced maternal attention.[7] If the children were closely spaced (9–18 months) or widely spaced (43 or more months) they received more attention. The least attention was shown to infants who were middle spaced, particularly those born 19–30 months after the birth of their next sibling. They think this may be because children close in age are treated more like one unit, so they all get similar attention, while those further apart are each like first children.

My first three children were each a year apart, and out of necessity, I did treat them as a unit. They ate at the same time, took their naps at the same time, and even bathed together. We all played the same game and I read them all the same book, usually at the level of my first-born. In this way, they did get the same attention. When my fourth child, Kelly, was born, four years after my third, I felt as though she were an only child.

The researchers also found that although the second children were held more than first-, third-, or fourth-born babies, they were smiled at less and played with less. Perhaps Mother is so conscious of the jealousy of her first child that she tries not to stimulate it by too much smiling and playing with the second. By the time the third child arrives she is over this fear and can be more openly affectionate. Also, the second time around is a quieter but more comfortable arrangement. Mother has played and cooed so much at her first child that she may be experiencing burnout with her second. She probably enjoys the quiet times with her baby, away from the constant questions and demands of her first child.

What happens to the second child because of this "benign neglect"? Dr. Alfred E. Fischer, a pediatrician, found that even if the second child is more agreeable and placid in the beginning, this preferential treatment of the first-born will arouse a feeling of "neglect" in the second child that will manifest later. Dr. Fischer found these symptoms appeared when the second child was generally between one and three years of age and learning to walk, talk, and develop various skills. "It is then," says Fischer, "that he begins to 'use the first born as his pacemaker with the ever present drive to overcome and surpass him.' "[8]

Once Shannon was about four months old, she became a much happier, more placid child and, like the women Fischer mentions, I took advantage of her ability to amuse herself. Therefore I was surprised when she began to have temper tantrums about eighteen months of age: the age, Fischer says, she probably became aware of her competition. Also, this was aggravated by the birth of her younger brother, Tom. She would follow me from room to room and throw herself forcefully on the floor, flailing her arms and legs and screaming loudly. My pediatrician had advised me to ignore her and simply move to another room. When I did this, she would follow me into that room and repeat her tantrum. After about a month of this, when she realized it would not get her the desired attention, she began a new tactic. She would attach herself to my leg, her chubby little hands clasped together, and hang on wherever I moved. I got used to doing dishes and other household chores with Shannon firmly secured to my leg. I wish I had known then that she was simply seeking some recognition from me and if I had given her the proper attention, she would not have needed such bizarre behavior.

Shannon was the middle child for five years, sandwiched in between two active boys. John and Shannon had a good relationship and could play together for hours peacefully. Tom always felt left out and, as he got older, began to interfere in their play time. Shannon became the buffer, the peacemaker between the two. As the boys grew, so did their conflicts, so she often withdrew to her own room to play. She would spend long hours alone in her room playing and talking to her dolls, coloring and doing sticker books. I was so relieved to have at least one child who needed such little supervision that I didn't think to wonder if the constant time alone was dangerous for her. I just assumed that if she was in her room and quiet, all was well. It is true that the squeaky wheel gets the grease and John and Tom did a lot of squeaking.

One day when I was cleaning out the toy box, I found a piece of paper covered with childlike black crayon scrawls. But there the likeness to a child ended. Several curse words were written there, and one sentence was especially puzzling. It said: "He makes her mean." I called my older three children to me and asked about the note. Of course they all denied ever having seen it and my mother, who was with me at the time, concluded that a neighbor child must have written it; it couldn't have been one of her grandchildren.

I dismissed the children, but deep in my being I had a strong impression Shannon had written that note. This did not come out of natural reasoning because Shannon would have been the least obvious candidate. She was nine years old at the time and a model child. She had become good, sweet, soft-spoken, and always obedient. I often said that if all my children were as good as Shannon I would have very little to do. I shelved the matter of the note in a corner of my mind, knowing nonetheless that it was far from settled.

In the meantime my husband and I were learning about the influence the devil and his minions, can have over believers. At that time, our church met in our home and the children were always exposed to all the teachings, either in the meetings or over the dinner table with one of our frequent guests. After one of these particular discussions, Shannon came to me and confessed that she had written the note. She said she had been too ashamed to admit it but since she was learning about the devil's opposition, she believed there was some connection. She also confessed that for many months she had been tormented by a "voice" telling her to throw herself out of the car or to do something violent to herself. The sentence that I remembered from the note, "He makes her mean," suddenly took on new relevance.

I called John at work and we decided to take her that evening to a church that had a special ministry in this area. That night

Shannon was freed from what we felt had become a demonic influence, including what the man praying for her called "a spirit of aloneness" that kept her isolated from other people, fed her lies that no one loved her, and even told her to commit suicide! He could not possibly have known the hours our nine-year-old spent alone in her room—hours I thought were not harmful. He told us that if we noticed her withdrawing too much again, we should take authority over Satan, and command the spirit of aloneness out of her in the name of Jesus, and we would not have any more problems. (Shannon was much better after that.)

Second children do, however, need time alone. They have a sensitive nature and too much stimulation can cause them problems. But, we parents must be careful not to allow them to withdraw into their rooms for long periods of time and not to assume (as I did) that there is nothing wrong in being alone. They need a healthy balance between fellowship and play with others and time alone. We will have to be sensitive to find out each one of our children's requisite needs in this area and then help them find the balance.

Some questions parents need to ask concerning their second child may be: Does he participate in outside activities? Does he seem happy and content? Where does he spend the majority of his time? Does he have a close friend or friends and do they spend sufficient time together? Often, we parents are so busy with our own concerns that we do not notice the child who keeps to himself. Instead, we just assume that all is well. Ask God to give you special insights into the unspoken needs of this often overlooked second child.

Besides the danger of spending too much time alone, we need to see that our second-borns do have some time alone to dream and recharge. As I mentioned earlier, second children, like Jacob, are often introverted. Unfortunately, many of us have the wrong idea of introversion: We picture a socially backward person who hates the company of others. Nothing could be further from the truth. You cannot always tell by a person's actions whether he is an extravert or an introvert. Introverts can be very social people. These two attitudes simply refer to the way a person receives energy. The extravert appears to be energized by people. Talking to people, playing with people, and working with people charges their batteries. Extraverts experience loneliness when they are not in contact with people. Introverts, on the other hand, seem to draw their energy from solitary activities—working quietly alone, reading, or participating in activities that involve few or no other people. They may love being with people at social gatherings but feel drained by constant interaction. They are likely to feel the most lonely in a crowd.

My oldest is definitely extraverted. During his first year of medical school he lived in an apartment by himself. He spent as little time as possible in the apartment and could never study there. He had to be in the library, surrounded by other students, or in a friend's apartment. After six months of living alone, John found a roommate and was much happier. Shannon, on the other hand, studies best when alone. She has lived alone for several years and loves it. The order could be reversed, with the oldest being the introvert and the second, the extravert. It is important that parents recognize this distinction in their children and help them to understand their basic needs for sociability and adjust to them. Since about seventy-five percent of the general population are extraverts, the introvert may feel there is something wrong with him. Parents should be able to reassure their introverted child that he is merely responding to the way God made him and his preference for time alone is just part of his basic temperament.

I am an introverted second child and my husband can tell immediately when I need time alone. He is an extraverted third child and can handle people around almost twenty-four hours a day. If I don't get some time alone, on the other hand, I begin to get irritated and edgy. At one time, this was one of the greatest sources of our marital problems, but now John understands that my need to be alone is not a sign of antisocial behavior. Once he recognizes the symptoms of being "peopled out," he helps me realize I need to say no to time with people and yes to time alone. I love to hear the "sounds of silence" as does my daughter Shannon but I thank God He gave me a sociable husband who keeps me from becoming too isolated from people.

Relationship with Parents

Whatever the first child is, the second will be just the opposite. This is called sibling deidentification, that is, an attempt to be unlike one's sibling. Along with emphasizing different character traits, first and second children often identify with opposite parents to further enforce their differences. One study found in two-child families that a higher proportion of second children felt close to the mother, while a higher proportion of first children felt close to the father.[9] This lines up with other studies that show Father is more actively involved with the first child than with later children.

If the parent likes himself and the qualities he sees mirrored in his child, there will be a good relationship. If, on the other hand, the parent dislikes that particular aspect of himself that the child represents, the relationship could be poor.

Although the greater proportion of second children feel closer to the mother, the sex of the child may be a stronger determining factor in parental preference. If the first child is a boy, for instance, and Mother maintains an intense preoccupation with this first-born, what is called cross-sex preference may occur—that is, the mother preferring a son and the father a second-born daughter. Or if the first-born girl is the father's favorite, her second-born brother may be the mother's. Dr. John McDermott says that when this happens, "when one child is the favorite of one parent and the other child the favorite of the other, the youngsters' personality characteristics will be exaggerated to please the parent who values them."[10]

This seemed to be the situation in my household as I was

growing up. My mother and older brother had a close relationship and I guess somewhere along the line I staked out my father. I was a middle child, and since my little sister seemed to have the edge in the feminine department, I became a tomboy. My memories of childhood revolve around playing softball, which I did all summer long, or playing the father while my little sister played the mother in our game of house. Later I developed an intense interest in horseback riding and guns; my father was proficient at both since he had been raised on a farm. I tried to become my father's boy and when he took me horseback riding or was teaching me to clean and load my own .22, I thought I had almost succeeded. It was not till many years later that I realized I was scared to death of horses and guns. All those years I had feigned an interest in those things I thought would please my father and yet, deep down, I was living a lie.

I realized that my own family continued this pattern. I retained a close relationship with John, while Shannon was just like her dad. Since Shannon has left home for college, I am surprised to see many characteristics emerging in her personality that are more like me than her father. Shannon had done the same thing I had. She had patterned herself after her father, in this case a laid-back third-born. Shannon is discovering that she is not as laid back as she once believed. She is a competitive middle child just like her mother but it took her exodus from home to set her free to discover her real identity.

There is another quality second-borns tend to have besides being placid, that of independence—a further result of both Mother and Father's increased confidence in their abilities with their second child. Irma Hilton conducted a study at Columbia University to study the effect of mother-child interactions.[11] She studied sixty mother-child pairs—twenty only children, twenty first-borns, and twenty second-borns. She set up an experiment where these sixty children, aged four, were asked to put a puzzle together in the presence of their mothers. The experimenter would then take the mother aside and tell her the child was doing well or that he was slower than most of the other children. After that, the experimenter would leave the room, supposedly to get the materials for the next test, but actually to allow observers to watch the mother and child through a one-way mirror.

It was found that a mother of a first-born or only child exhibited a higher incidence of demonstrative love when her child was doing well, and if the child was doing poorly she exhibited a significant decrease in her level of verbal support. The second-born's mother was less extreme in her demonstrations of love, more consistent in showing her love, and not as critical if her child was failing. The mother of the first-born and of the only child "rejected" her child by withdrawing love when he failed—a message made all the more powerful because she gave excessive demonstrations of love when he succeeded. Also, the mothers of first and only children were much more interfering even when they had been told to sit quietly.

This example of the constant interference and inconsistency a mother shows her first-born helps explain why the first child is more dependent than the second. He never knows what to expect since his mother's reactions are so extreme. He does not learn to set his own goals, but rather to achieve the ones set for him.

When my children were small I would have said that this study didn't hold true for my first and second children. John seemed to be the more independent while Shannon was a shy, retiring child. The first indication I had that the surface traits may not show the whole picture was when I decided to enroll them in nursery school. Shannon was three at the time and John was four. I was a little worried about Shannon's ability to adjust as she was so placid and withdrawn but was sure the presence of her brother would be a comfort. Imagine my surprise when I came to pick them up the first day and saw Shannon happily at play with several children while John was sitting red-eyed, anxiously watching the door for my return. When, after a week, John had not adjusted any better I took both of them out of school.

Many years later when the matter of college came up, John chose a school close to home, while Shannon decided to go to Arizona State two thousand miles away, where she did not know one person. The authors of *First Child, Second Child . . .* found that the second child, especially if the middle of three, has a tendency to leave home early in life. In fact, they say "that your capacity to make your way in the larger world before your sibs dared to venture out constitutes a unique strength. This strength, incidentally, is characteristic of your birth order and yours alone."[12]

So don't be surprised if your second child shows a much more independent streak than your first. Your consistency of calm response has made him more stubbornly courageous.

This stubborn independence, though, presents a problem when it comes to discipline. Just as parents relaxed in their expectations of the second child, they also relaxed in the area of discipline. In a 1952 questionnaire, researchers found that "physical punishment was administered to first offspring half again as frequently as to second offspring, and thumb-sucking was permitted twice as frequently in the second-born."[13] The first child receives much more disciplinary action from the parents and is capable of taking a lot more pressure. His need for parental approval makes him more sensitive to correction. A second-born is not. He is not looking for parental approval and has less to lose. He may withdraw under that pressure, or rebel. I know of instances in which a father with a first-born daughter and second son has put pressure on the second son to accept the responsibility of a first child. In doing this, he has caused the son to withdraw from the pressure or else to attempt to fill the role at the cost of his own inner peace.

Frank was a second child and only son of a strong, achieving first-born father. His father was the owner of a successful construction company and Frank, his only son, was slotted to follow in his father's rather large footprints. Frank did manage outwardly to become the achieving, successful person his father desired and eventually took over the firm. Inside, however, he was a nervous, unhappy man who couldn't seem to enjoy life. When he realized he was playing the role of a first son while his inner second-born nature longed to have less responsibility, he sold the company and went to work for someone else. Today, he has learned to enjoy life and leave the worries to his first-born boss.

Of course you have to discipline your second child, not only for his own sake but because your first child is looking on and waiting to see what you are going to do. Most of the mothers I have talked to have said they are most intimidated by their second child in the area of discipline. This child when disciplined responds one of two ways: either throws a tremendous temper tantrum or is so terribly "hurt" by the correction that the mother is left feeling guilty for injuring her sensitive child. As a result, Mother is so intimidated by what the reaction might be that she tiptoes around the second child, and the child, as a result, learns to play on Mother's feelings.

What's the answer then? In the next chapter we are going to consider the motivations and fears of the second-born, why he responds so negatively to correction, and what parents can do about it.

Parenting Pointers

1. After the birth of the second child, Father should assume more care of the first-born to help ease the lack of attention the child receives from Mother.

2. Do not allow your baby to cry without responding, even if that response is delayed.

3. Try to spend time alone with your second child.

4. Stimulate your second child by talking and playing with him.

5. Make sure you know your children's preference for introversion or extraversion. Help them find the healthy balance between time alone and fellowship with friends.

6. Recognize that your second child will be more independent than your first and you cannot pressure him into doing what you want.

Eight

The Sensitive Child

I had invited about twenty mothers of two or more children to meet to discuss their second child. After I finished giving them a rundown of some of the research and also my own personal experience, a few of the women asked questions about problems they were having with their second child. I noticed one woman, Sally, looking more and more perplexed. Finally she spoke up.

"You know, I don't relate to any of these problems that you have mentioned. My second child is the sweetest and best child of my four."

"How old is she?" Yvonne asked.

"She's ten."

"Just wait," was Yvonne's laughing response.

Everyone in the room responded immediately, each one wanting to tell of her own personal experience with that puzzling second child.

100

What is there about the second child that is so confusing and why do mothers seem to find their second child more intimidating than any of the others? All of the mothers seemed in agreement that their second child seemed almost schizophrenic at times. "One minute she will be angry and rebellious and then, within a short period of time, the sweetest of all my children," seemed to be a description that was often repeated.

One of the mothers said she calls her son "the cactus kid" because, in her words, "he can be so prickly and tough to get close to. But at other times he is sweet and affectionate." Since this seemed to be a constantly recurring theme, we decided to discuss the reasons for this "double-minded" type of behavior.

A Wounded Spirit

Every mother I have ever talked to about her second child has said that this child is the most sensitive. This seemingly didn't fit in with most of the research on first and second children: It was the first child who was designated as the "sensitive" child. Then I began asking what they meant by sensitive. It is true that the first child is the most sensitive to parental approval, but every mother without fail said her second child is the most sensitive or reactive to criticism or correction. This seemed to hold true whether the child was the second and youngest or second of three or more.

"Even when I am trying to build up my son and encourage him, he finds some way to twist it into something negative," said one frustrated mother.

"I find the same thing," said another. "It's so bad that sometimes I'm afraid to say anything to him."

My mind was filled with memories of my own mother trying to talk to me and my stomping off to my room in anger to sulk and pout at what I thought was her destructive criticism. I carried this same attitude into my marriage and the slightest hint of criticism from my husband could send me into a three-day depression.

Shannon followed in my footsteps. One Friday evening she

was sulking around the house because she had had a disagreement with a friend and had nowhere to go that night. Her father was trying to help her see that she needed to reach out more to people and not to wait passively for them to come to her. He made the mistake of saying, "Now Kelly [her sister five years younger] doesn't get upset if one of her friends is busy. She just calls another one."

With that Shannon burst into tears and ran up to her room screaming, "I can't be like Kelly! I am not Kelly!" Poor John. He sat there completely mystified, mumbling, "That's not what I meant at all."

Why is it that second children are so sensitive? The first, as we have seen, directs his energy outward, and also is capable of taking a lot more parental pressure without collapsing under it. The second directs his energy inward and is more introverted in his thinking. (Remember that this is true even though the second may *appear* to be more social and friendly than the first.) This introverted approach to life results in a more sensitive spirit—a spirit that will "take in" whatever is interpreted as criticism—a cross look from Mother, a joking remark by a sibling, or the gruff reply of a busy father. Then, because of his introverted thinking pattern, the second child cannot throw these off the way the first child can, and he begins to dwell on them. The result is a wounded spirit, wounded by what he interprets as criticism or rejection.

Proverbs 18:14 says, "The spirit of a man will sustain his infirmity; but a wounded spirit who can bear?" (KJV). It appears that it is easier for a man to suffer illness than to suffer from a wounded spirit. The sensitive, second child often suffers a wounded spirit and, as a result, becomes very reactive to criticism.

Forgiveness

One of the greatest challenges for the parents of a second-born child is to guard that child against a wounded spirit. One way to do this is to teach the child early the value of forgiveness. Because a sensitive person is more easily wounded, he therefore tends to build up unforgiveness. Second children seldom forgive and, many mothers assured me, they *never* forget. We need to begin early, then, teaching these children what unforgiveness will do to them and helping them to realize that they will be the losers if they do not forgive.

One of the first things God did in my life as a new Christian was to teach me about forgiveness not only through the words of Jesus in the Gospels but also through a book called *None of These Diseases*. Dr. S. I. McMillen, the author, explains in medical terms the detrimental things that happen to us physically when we refuse to forgive. Since I had suffered many of those same physical ailments, I decided it was too high a price to pay and so asked God to reveal to me all those I needed to forgive and release. It took about a year to work through all the forgiveness. Names and circumstances would come to mind from situations that had happened even in grammar school. Every time I remembered and prayed to forgive, I got a little freer.

Many second children are unaware of the unforgiveness they carry because they are used to repressing their emotions. It would be a good idea for the mother to be aware of any situation in her second child's life that is causing unforgiveness and to spend time praying with the child to forgive and release the person(s) involved. I try to help my children understand the situation from the other person's perspective and this way it is easier for them to forgive. We should begin with an acknowledgement of their hurt—"I know you were deeply hurt by what happened to you"—and in this way convey that we understand what they are feeling. Then it will be easier to explain to them their need to forgive to protect themselves from the effects of bitterness.

Correction or Criticism

Another way of protecting our second children from a wounded spirit is to pray for wisdom when correcting them. We need to let them know that, while we disapprove of their behavior, we are not rejecting them. I was reading an article recently about British Prime Minister Margaret Thatcher, who is a second child. It said, "Though Margaret can be *deeply hurt by personal criticism,* attacks on her policies usually make her dig her heels in all the harder"[1] (italics mine). All second children can be deeply hurt by what they perceive as personal criticism so we need to be careful how we approach them with correction. We are used to being very vocal with the first child and wrongly assume the second can take the same treatment. Even though we try to be diplomatic in our criticism of our second-borns, there will be those times when they are going to twist what we say and turn it into a rejection. This goes along with the second child's motto that "a good offense is the best defense." My poor mother said the reason she didn't discipline me as much as my older brother was because I was so sensitive. Evidently my reactions worked to keep my mother feeling intimidated and guilty.

Parents, and mothers especially, need to find the balance between protecting their child's spirit and bringing needed correction. Consistent firmness and refusal to be intimidated seem to be the key. If our children learn their reactions will put us off, they will always have the upper hand. At the same time, we need to learn how to help them change wrong behavior patterns without attacking their character.

When a child responds in anger to correction we cannot back down or meet that anger with greater anger of our own. Our anger is just more fuel for the fire. Instead, we need to stand our ground and say something like: "Julie, I am not going to be put off by your hysterics. I don't want you to suffer later in life because I didn't love you enough to correct you. Now calm down and listen to what I am going to say." If they know we are not intimidated by them, they will respond to our firmness. Then, we can put our arms around them and reassure them of our love. By this time they are usually ready to listen to what we tell them.

Embarrassment

One of the biggest problems that came out in our discussion with the mothers who gathered to discuss the second child was the problem of this child's exaggerated fear of embarrassment. Evidently second children are more prone to embarrassment than any other child in the birth-order constellation. One of the ways they deal with it is to try to learn all the rules and etiquette of any situation so they won't look like the "odd man out."

Many second children deal with this problem by showing exaggerated attention to their clothing. If they dress correctly, they feel they can avoid any sort of embarrassment. The mothers who met with me that day related many stories of unused clothing hanging in the closets of their second children because someone had made a remark about it.

"That must be it," said Jeannie. "One time someone made a derogatory remark about my son's brand-new sweater and he has never worn it since."

I often say that I can pick out a second child in a roomful of people. Frequently they are the best dressed in the group with all the perfectly matching accessories. This is only one tactic of the second child to avoid embarrassment.

The mother of "the cactus kid" said her son shied from embarrassment in the opposite way by refusing to get new clothes or a haircut. She said, "He hates to get anything new that will call attention to himself." She recently bought him several new shirts but he would only wear one about every two weeks so that no one would realize he had new clothes.

One situation that still stands out clearly in my mind, although it happened more than thirty years ago, occurred when I went grocery shopping with my mom. She was getting her groceries checked out while I waited for the cart to be loaded. Evidently the girl rang up the wrong price on an article and my mother, in a loud voice, started to question her. I can remember praying for the ground to open up and swallow me as I saw heads turning in

our direction. I spent most of my life trying to avoid embarrassment and here was my own mother deliberately bringing it on.

After I shared on this aspect of embarrassment, one of the
mothers went home and asked her second-born daughter if she
ever felt embarrassed by her. "Was I surprised when she listed
about ten incidents in a few minutes," she told me later. "I was
even more surprised that she remembered each one and probably
has not forgiven me."

Parents need to guard the spirits of their children by protecting
them from embarrassment. Even though the second child is
especially prone to embarrassment, it can affect any child in the
family. Mothers should never insist their children dress in a way
that is obviously different from the other children. While we all
hope our children will grow up and learn not to be unduly
influenced by peers, it is unfair to expect a young child to stand
up against this pressure. As long as there is nothing immoral
about their clothing such as a skimpy outfit or a T-shirt with an
obscene saying, we should allow them to dress like their peers.
Also parents should never reprimand a child in front of his friends.
It is one of the most destructive things we can do. If we see them
doing something that needs to be corrected, we should take them
aside and tell them. They will appreciate our understanding and
be more responsive to the correction.

When I would go to my children's school occasionally in my capacity as room mother or some other function, I would always respect my children's admonitions: "Now Mom, don't crack any of
your corny jokes" or "Don't give me any extra attention" and most
emphatically, "Don't kiss me in front of the other kids." Fortunately I realized that their tender little spirits were at stake and never
considered their requests silly. My husband often went to the junior
high school to teach a health class on dentistry. He said that often
one of the children would walk by him in the hall without even acknowledging him. He was wise enough not to make a scene or mention it to him. Now we can laugh together with them about these
issues—but then it was no laughing matter.

Intimidation

Perhaps the awareness of this sensitive spirit is what makes parents tiptoe around their second child. Even though I am a second child myself, I realized one day that I was intimidated by Shannon. I was more natural in my responses with the other children—if I was angry I showed it and didn't try to water it down—but with Shannon I was much less spontaneous. One mother stated it exactly when she said, "It's just that you don't want to rock the boat."

Also, the fact that the second child can be the sweetest child in the family or the most disagreeable also keeps parents off guard. Many of the mothers had similar experiences with their second child as the agreeable child, the placid one, and then around twelve years of age turning intense, almost hyperactive.

This was my experience and it must have been hard for my mother to adjust to the change. She said that I was shy and retiring when I was young. I would even run and hide under the bed when company came to the house. One mother of a second-born boy said that he always pinched her when people visited. My own second child just stood holding onto my leg and screaming until the company left. My mother tells me I was so introverted that she thought I might need counseling, but when I entered high school my personality did an abrupt turnaround.

My older brother was gifted in several areas and it was not until I entered high school that I saw a way to compete. High school is a closed social system with its own rules for acceptance. Even though my brother got straight A's, could play the piano, and was a creative writer, all anyone cared about was what and how many organizations you belonged to. At last I had found my niche. By the time I graduated from high school I was voted the friendliest girl in the senior class and was vice-president (good job for a second child) of many school organizations and also of the senior class. In four years I changed from a placid, introverted child to a hyperactive, competitive, and somewhat rebellious person.

I could never imagine my second child becoming as competitive and rebellious as I was in high school and college. We had a close relationship and it was difficult for me when she entered eighth grade and just closed up. It was as if the drawbridge to her inner castle had swung shut and a sign was nailed up that said: *No visitors.* She remained "closed" for four years, her way of being rebellious, and then in her senior year of high school began to open up again. There were many times during those four years that I wanted to force her to open up to me but that still, small voice of the Holy Spirit always seemed to say: "Just love her and accept her." So I tried to stifle my desire to make her communicate and just show her love and acceptance. The first year after she left for college God totally restored our relationship and I was glad I didn't try to push my way in.

Because of their sensitivity to slights, second children may become extremely private about themselves. A recent article about Robert R. McCormick stated: "Robert R. McCormick's *passion for privacy* was so intense that it has taken 30 years to penetrate the public image of the man who owned, edited and published The Chicago Tribune for much of the 20th Century"[2] (italics mine). Robert McCormick was (as I'm sure you have guessed) a second child. This secrecy, and the emotional guard that second children put up, hides their tremendous vulnerability. Parents need to be aware of this and realize that to push and pry into their second child's life will only result in the drawbridge being closed more tightly. I can sit and pull out my other children through conversation but my second has to be willing to initiate the discussion. To do this they have to know they can trust us.

Here again, the second child presents a paradox: withdrawn and suspicious one minute and then overly trusting and vulnerable the next. This is in large part because their big brother or sister is alternately a hero one minute and an enemy the next. The child has mixed feelings and responds accordingly. No wonder Mom and Dad end up somewhat confused about their second child. Just about the time they are ready to strangle him, he becomes a different person.

Pressure

I mentioned that it is useless to pressure a second child. Pressure will cause the child to rebel or become discouraged. One mother mentioned that she often pressured her second-born daughter to study more and to do more around the house. She said that under pressure her daughter became nonfunctional, which she always interpreted as rebellion and consequently applied more pressure. She said her results failed ninety-nine percent of the time to reach the desired goal.

Besides the normal pressure of everyday life, second-borns are great at putting pressure on themselves to achieve and this pressure causes anxiety and anger to begin to build up. At some point, when the pressure becomes unbearable, the second child will either explode in anger and release the pressure that way, or retreat into doing nothing. This tendency will continue into adulthood so parents need to help their second children develop more constructive ways to handle pressure. One effective way is through physical activity.

All my life I have had a deep love for physical exercise but didn't realize why until I saw a pattern developing. Whenever I was too busy to take time out of my schedule for recreation, the anxiety caused by the pressure of my schedule landed me in a depression. Then by becoming nonproductive for a period of time, I eased my way out of the pressure. Once I realized this I began to work off my anxiety through a physical activity; I made that a priority.

I have imparted this lesson to my own second child, who is the only one of the four with a definite need in this area. I can always tell when she is starting to let pressure control her. She becomes edgy and irritable and her normally relaxed manner disappears. She has learned to recognize this herself and has taken up jogging as a way of handling her pressure. We have both learned that when we feel anxious and burdened the best thing to do is to drop everything and go for a walk, bike ride, or jog. The hour or so spent in activity is certainly worth it since we prevent ourselves from becoming nonfunctional for a longer period of time.

Parents need to direct their second children into physical activity early in life so that they can establish good habits of working off anger and tension. Probably one of the worst jobs for a second-born would be in an office with a lot of pressure. Second-born men love to work outside or in occupations where they can spend time with people. Unlike big brother or sister, relationships are more important than achievement to them.

One father of a second-born son recently told us how his son withdrew from a pressure he was finding too heavy. His son was in the last quarter of his junior year in medical school. Without any warning or discussion, he dropped out of school and thereby forfeited three years of hard work. He told his father he was tired of living up to others' expectations of him. The truth was that others had not put excessive pressure or expectations on him; this was a pressure he had put on himself. If he could have been alerted to the danger and then taken measures to alleviate the pressure, he probably could have stayed in school. But he reacted in a typical second-born way: He let the pressure build to gigantic proportions and then bailed out.

Karl König says that the second child "likes to live without making too much effort. Existence does not only mean sweat and labour; it is joy and bliss, experience and wonder."[3] The first child may be a workaholic but the second cannot take the constant pressure of work without any recreation. One second-born dentist friend of ours finds an outlet from his intense, detailed work through chopping wood and doing yardwork. In this way he can work off the strain of the tension he is under and still enjoy the wonders of the outdoors.

One other way you can help your second child with the pressure is by getting him to talk it out. As I mentioned earlier, it won't be easy because second children often resist what they feel is prying. The parent is going to have to establish trust with the child and take the time to gently lead the child into the discovery of what is bothering him. A good idea might be to spend some time alone with that child, perhaps going out to eat or even going for a walk. In the normal flow of the conversation, the second child will usually begin to work out the problem.

Remember: Even though a second-born can be stubborn, as we will see in the next chapter, in a pressure situation he is not being stubborn by not talking—he doesn't know what's bothering him. Because of the introverted nature of the second child, he buries most of his thoughts and feelings and probably isn't even aware of them. My husband was the one who got me to begin to talk out what I was feeling. I didn't even know when I was angry. I used to say I felt frustrated. One night my husband replied, "You don't feel frustrated, you are angry." I realized he was right and with his help was able to trace down the root of my anger. It may take awhile to get your second child talking, but stick with it. Once they get started they usually will go on for a long time. Often, when Shannon is feeling pressured, I will send her to talk to one of the young married women in the fellowship who has a good listening ear and keen gift of discernment. Shannon will always return from these talks with a sense of lightness and freedom.

The Root of Rejection

A person with a sensitive spirit is more open to rejection than the average person. Although every person suffers rejection from time to time in the process of growing up, to the second child rejection is an intimate part of his nature. All the personality traits of the second child that we have covered in this chapter—extreme sensitivity to slights and correction, embarrassment, privacy, emotional distance from people, and an unforgiving spirit—point to a root problem of rejection resulting from a wounded spirit.

These are tactics the second child learns to prevent himself from being vulnerable and suffering any more rejection. The way second children have of twisting everything, even loving correction, into a rejection reveals the root.

Even though I manifested all of these personality traits as a second child, I was a Christian for about seven years before I realized I had a deep problem with rejection. By this time I was forty years old and had developed many great coping devices. About twice a year, though, an argument with my husband would seem to stir the sleeping creature within me, and I would find myself helpless to squelch it. I would stay on the verge of tears or anger, and my mind would be filled with thoughts of self-hate and hatred toward everyone close to me. This was quite embarrassing to me since my husband and I were in a Christian leadership capacity and I was supposed to be a mature Christian. I would literally go into hiding until the attack passed.

Finally, God delivered me sovereignly from what we believed was a demonic spirit of rejection. I was alone at the time as I had refused to go with my family to the July 4th fireworks demonstration. I was sobbing and feeling like a failure as a Christian and a wife and mother. As I cried out to God for help, I suddenly felt as if a giant root were being pulled out of the innermost part of my stomach. As soon as it was out, my crying simply stopped, and I was filled with an overwhelming sense of freedom and joy. God had taken away, in a matter of seconds, the pain and inordinate sense of failure that had plagued me for years. That was seven years ago and I have never since that time had one of my "spells."

One thing I saw clearly after this experience was how my thinking had gotten twisted during those times. It was as if the words people had spoken to me didn't come straight into my mind. Instead they followed a tortuous labyrinth until, when they were finally fed back to me, they had a different meaning. I saw them now as words of rejection and hurt, even though they had been spoken by people I knew loved me. One of the greatest freedoms in the last seven years is the freedom to receive personal correction in the spirit it is given. I no longer react to *perceived* criticism and am able therefore to be a lot more vulnerable to people since I do not constantly have to protect myself from real or imagined rejection.

One of the ways parents can help their second child or any of their children who suffer from rejection is to help them to strengthen their minds. Paul tells us to take "every thought captive to the obedience of Christ" (2 Corinthians 10:5, NAS). We need to help our children see that they cannot accept any negative thoughts that Satan might attempt to put into their minds such as: Your mother and father don't really love you; you will always be a failure; your sister is much prettier than you. They need to understand that every one of these thoughts, if accepted, gives ground to the enemy—ground that he will use to his advantage and our disadvantage. I believe the reason God did not free me from the spirit of rejection earlier was that I had never fought against these thoughts but was a willing recipient. I had never strengthened my mind against the enemy. Until I learned to do that God could not deliver me because I would have come right back under bondage at the first lie that Satan whispered in my ear. If we can help our children understand these concepts, we can prevent many of these problems in their lives.

You and your second child could also do a Bible study on the rejection that Jesus endured, not only from His entire generation but also from His Father (Isaiah 53:3; Luke 17:25; and Mark 15:34). You could point out that Jesus willingly accepted that rejection so that we wouldn't have to be afflicted, and that by believing Satan's lies we are letting him steal the victory Jesus won for us. You also might spend some time studying passages that emphasize Jesus' promises to us that He will never reject or forsake us, such as Deuteronomy 31:6,8; 1 Samuel 12:22; Isaiah 42:16; and Hebrews 13:5–6. When one of my children is having a problem in a particular area, I will usually write out a Scripture pertaining to that problem for him or her to memorize. Kelly often had trouble falling asleep, so I would tape Scripture passages next to her bed so that she could meditate on them as she went to sleep. We need to teach our children to fight their weaknesses with the Word of God and turn them into strengths.

We have focused so much on the problems of the second child in this chapter that you may be wondering what will happen to this child in adulthood. Is he doomed to go through life forever protecting his sensitive spirit, keeping his distance from those who might hurt him, and never reaching his potential? Of course the answer is no, and in the next chapter, concluding this section on the second-born, we will see some additional traits—performance and character—of the second child and how this child can use these to enhance his particular spiritual gifts in the Kingdom of God.

Parenting Pointers

1. Teach your second child about forgiveness and take the time to pray with him when he has been offended. Explain how unforgiveness can even affect us physically.

2. Refuse to be intimidated by your second child. Approach correction with firmness and love and do not let him throw a temper tantrum or withdraw from you. Reassure your child of your love and acceptance of him after correction.

3. Guard your child's sensitive spirit by protecting him from embarrassment. Don't insist he dress in a way that is obviously different from the other children and never reprimand him in front of others.

4. Honor his need for privacy. Do not try to pry information out of him but rather create a trusting relationship that will allow him to open up. Remember he needs a lot of acceptance.

5. Teach your second child to deal with pressure through physical activity. Help him develop the habit of going for a walk or bike ride when he feels anxious or pressured.

6. In a relaxed, no-pressure situation, encourage your second-born to talk about his day. Do not interrupt with correction but let him express just what he is feeling.

7. Help him to strengthen his mind against rejection by first recognizing Satan's tactics and secondly by memorizing appropriate Scriptures on God's love and acceptance of us.

Nine

The Prophets

While it is true that first and second children will almost always have opposite traits, there is also an identification that occurs within siblings. That is

> the process by which one child sees himself in the other, experiences life vicariously through the behavior of the other, and begins to expand on possibilities for himself by learning through a brother's or sister's experience. . . . Identification is the "glue" of the sibling relationship.[1]

The researchers who studied this identification warn, however, that differentiation also has to take place between brothers and sisters. Otherwise they say a "dangerous process of fusion can block the growth of each child." If one child is not able to see areas of his competency, he might try to imitate an older brother or sister and not be able to develop on his own. This need for individuality is one reason why it is important for parents to try to discern each child's differences and capabilities and then direct them appropriately.

Another reason, closely related, is that the child is primed for a life of discouragement if he tries to copy another child who is more gifted.

This was the reason I experienced my first major failure at eight years of age. My older brother, Tom, had been taking piano lessons for three years and was in the words of his teacher "a budding concert pianist." He was not only nimble-fingered and quick to learn; he also had perfect pitch. So, when I got to the same age that my brother had started his lessons, it just seemed natural that I should continue the musical tradition. Evidently the supply of musical talent in our family ran out after the birth of my brother because I was a dismal failure. It was hard to watch the expectant anticipation vanish slowly from my teacher's eyes as the weeks went on. Finally, she confided to my mother that perhaps my talent lay in other areas.

It was years before I would ever attempt to do anything that I thought my brother could do better than I. When I was in high school, I expressed an interest in painting and my mother enrolled me in the Art Institute of Chicago. This was finally something I could do all by myself—neither my sister nor my brother had ever shown any interest in art.

If your first child is artistic, you might direct your second into some kind of sports activity. One child might like to play the piano while another might prefer drums (usually a younger child who likes to make his presence known). Whatever you do, don't put them in the same activity; it will be impossible to avoid comparison and one child will always come off the loser. It may mean more trips in the car and a fuller schedule, but in the long run it will be worth it.

Second children will differ not only in performance traits; they have two unique character traits as well. They will be more stubborn than the first and more down-to-earth in the area of intelligence.

Stubbornness

Second children can be notoriously stubborn. Once they get their heels dug in the ground, watch out. You won't budge them. Much of this stubbornness comes from the interaction of the second child with his older sibling. Researchers found similarities between first and second children at both the child and the college level in their responses to power.

> All firstborn perceived themselves and were perceived by second born as exercising higher power—that is, they commanded, reprimanded, scolded, and bossed. Reciprocally, the second born pleaded, whined, sulked, and appealed for help and sympathy from the firstborn and others . . . . The firstborn also gave more rewards and deprived the second born of more privileges. The second born responded by *getting angry, being stubborn,* and by harassing, pestering, and bothering the firstborn[2] (italics mine).

The second child carries these same qualities into adulthood and if threatened may explode in anger or just retreat into stubborn silence.

Another reason for the stubbornness of the second child is rooted in the childhood family. The schedule of most families revolves around the first child. Dr. Ruth Lesser, a New York psychoanalyst, says, "The family fits in with the first child, but the second child has to fit in with the family."[3] I made sure that Shannon, and later Tom, both took their naps at John's naptime so that I would have a few minutes of quiet. Once John started school, the others got fed as soon as John was taken care of and his lunch prepared. He was the first with activities and lessons, so we all got into the car and drove him to guitar lessons, Indian guides, or whatever other activity was in order that day. The oldest continues to control the environment as he grows by taking charge of it. The only way the second child has to fight this control is by saying no. And so he says it—often.

Another more subtle way of fighting the first-born is by developing a disdain for those things that delight every oldest child. Since first children love schedules, lists, being on time, and saving things, second children develop a "who cares?" attitude toward life. This often shows up in adulthood as procrastination, a dislike of details, and an inability to save anything, but especially money.

Parenthetically, in a marriage relationship I believe the second-born partner should automatically hand over the responsibility of the finances to his spouse unless the spouse is also a second-born. Then I would suggest hiring an accountant. It will be the best investment you can make! Some years ago when our congregation was learning about the authority structure in the home (Ephesians 5:22–6:9), we decided all the men should take care of their family's budgets. This worked quite well except, interestingly, in the case of second-born men. After six months of unpaid bills and coming to the verge of bankruptcy, the wives of these men asked if it would be all right if they took back the handling of the budget. The wives resumed their responsibility and within a short time their credit rating went up once more.

Intelligence

Research indicates that first-born children are more likely than others to achieve advanced university degrees and to excel in such intellectual professions as science, psychology, medicine, and college teaching.[4] The pages of Who's Who seem to be dominated by only children and first-born sons.[5] It was this phenomenon that first alerted Galton, an English scientist, to the birth order effect. He found a preponderance of first and only sons among eminent British scientists.

In a study of the personalities of first and second children, the adjective that showed up most frequently in describing the second child was "not studious."[6] As I mentioned earlier, the second will usually be just the opposite of the first and if the first develops in the usual serious, studious way, this would be expected. But there are other factors that predispose the second child to this trait.

Dr. Leon Yarrow of the National Institute of Child Health and Human Development has written, "Perhaps the most striking finding is the extent to which mother's stimulation influences developmental progress during the first six months. Its amount and quality are highly related to her baby's IQ."[7] In a study of attentiveness of the mother to the child, it was found that "the most attentive mothers had the most explorative infants. . . . Also, the babies who had received the most attention vocalized nearly three times as much as did the babies who received the least attention."[8]

If you remember the study in chapter seven, researchers found it was the second child who received the least stimulation in the area of smiling and playfulness. No wonder the second child is not as motivated as the first. If mothers can be aware of this tendency, they can take proper steps to ensure their second child will not suffer a loss of this type of stimulation. Also, "the single behavior most highly related to children's competency was verbal stimulation. It was especially important in helping the child to understand and to express language."[9] I can remember many times when I would be feeding Shannon while fielding John's many questions. So, even though I held Shannon for long periods of time (the only area in which second children come out first), my attention was on John. Perhaps mothers can alleviate this problem by spending time with their second children when the first is napping or in the evening after his bedtime.

My second child had a habit of waking up about 5:30 A.M. and not wanting to go back to sleep after her bottle. John didn't get up till about 8:00 A.M. and so I did have that early morning time alone with her. At that time I didn't see it as an advantage—I just wanted to go back to bed—but I can see it provided her with a special time where she had me all to herself. About the time she was ready for her morning nap, John would be getting up for breakfast, so he also had me alone first thing in the morning.

Just because the second child may not be as studious as the first, however, doesn't mean that the second is doomed to failure in school. Often the second child may be quicker than the first. The first may be consistent and a plodder while the second may be able to do well with little studying. Alfred Adler found that the

> second child is often more talented and successful than the first. Here we cannot suggest that heredity has any part in this development. If he goes ahead faster, it is because he trained more. Even when he is grown up and outside the family circle, he often makes use of a pacemaker; compares himself with some one whom he thinks more advantageously placed and tries to go beyond him.[10]

So the first child ahead of him may be the motivating factor in spurring that second child on to achieve. A magazine interviewer once asked Joan Rivers, "Where do you get your drive?" Joan replied, "From being the second child and a fat child. My sister was prettier, smarter and better than I was in every way."[11] In this situation her pacemaker proved to be the key to her success while with other second-borns such a successful first-born might have brought discouragement and defeat. Then, in order to cope, a second child may become extremely rebellious. In fact, research has shown that the second child will be the extremist in the family—either the best behaved or the most rebellious.

Is your second child competitive or "laid back"? If laid back then you might have to do some investigating to find an area that he can achieve in different from his older sibling. Second children have been found to be the most creative ones in the family. This was found in two-, three- and four-child families.[12] Try to discover your second child's special area of creativity and then point him in that direction. Even if he never becomes a Picasso, at least you will be stimulating him to find his special creative talents and this may be the key to stimulating him to achieve in other areas as well.

For instance, a second child's love of athletics can be used as a good motivational tool to get that "non-studious" second child to study. One friend of ours says that the only reason her second son strives to get good grades is so he can stay on the football, basketball, and baseball teams. He is a fine athlete but not interested in the traditional school subjects. Between his mother, coaches, and his love of sports, however, he is constantly being stimulated to study and achieve.

Second and later children do have it over the first child in one area: common sense. The first child learns from his parents while second and later children learn from their peers. First children are intellectually smart while later children are "street smart." The first child is often like the "absent-minded professor," his head in the clouds trying to work out some intricate formula but forgetting to wear matching socks. The important thing is recognizing that one kind of knowledge is not better than the other but simply equips the child for different functions in life. And we, as parents, are the ones who need to direct our children into those areas of life most in line with their talents and abilities and which will give the child the greatest satisfaction.

Dr. Dorothy Gross, director of the Program in Infant and Parent Development at the Bank Street College of Education in New York City, sums up the future of the second child when she states:

Competency doesn't just mean attending Harvard, and then going on to have ulcerative colitis or a heart attack. It also means relating well to other people, going to a job and not being consumed by it, truly enjoying yourself and your family. It means taking pleasure in the world, not just in how much money you can make. In this broader sense, second children show a lot of competence.[13]

Spiritual Gifts

Now for the gifts this second child is especially suited for.

Sensitivity to Others

In the last chapter we discussed the sensitive spirit of the second child and his resultant sensitivity to hurts, criticism, and correction. In addition to this, Alfred Adler says that the attitude of the second child has "a dominant note of being slighted, neglected, in it."[14] However, this sensitivity to slights does not have to be negative—it can be a strength. For instance, the second child is also sensitive to the slights and feelings of others. Every mother I talked to mentioned that it was her second child who was the most aware of what she was feeling. One mother recalled a day when she was lying across the bed trying to get rid of a migraine headache. It was her second son who came in to see if she was all right and then proceeded to take off her shoes so she could be more comfortable and get a cool washcloth for her head. The other two children didn't show nearly the concern of this child and yet he was also the one who could most intimidate her.

Besides being sensitive to other people, second children have a sensitivity to God. They seem to have the ability to hear and respond to God in a way that other children do not. Don't be fooled by the emotional wall they erect around themselves. When the Holy Spirit is ready to tear it down it will topple like the walls of Jericho. One of the first reactions of people to me after I was born again was: "I didn't like you before because you always seemed so aloof and distant. But you are so different now." Once Jesus came into my heart, I wasn't afraid of my vulnerability.

Justice

Because second children carry that "dominant note of being slighted" with them, they are children who are concerned with justice being done. Since they felt cheated, they are going to make sure no one else is cheated. They are sensitive to any real or imagined injustice and usually root for the underdog.

One mother related a problem that her fourth-grade son, Jonathan, was having in school. He was so concerned with justice that he would take up the offenses of other children in the class. This mainly occurred at recess during supervised kickball games. The teacher found herself taking longer and longer each day explaining, defining, and refining the rules before they went outside to play so that Jonathan would understand her rulings in the game. My friend and her husband talked to Jonathan and impressed on him that his actions constituted a greater unfairness than any unfairness perpetrated during the game since he was in a sense ruling the whole class. He could accept this logic and became more cooperative.

One strength his mother mentioned in this desire for justice was that Jonathan accepts the Word of God as final authority. She said that if she and her husband can show him a Scripture that bears on any situation at hand, he will accept God's point of view. It's almost as if the Supreme Court has made a decision and that decision is final. Perhaps this would be the best way for parents to challenge wrong behavior in their second children— find a Scripture and help them understand it.

The Prophets

The personality traits we have just discussed—sensitivity to people, sensitivity to God, concern with justice, recognizing Scripture as the final authority, and concern for the underdog— all describe a person with the motivation of a prophet. Even the stubbornness of the second child can be a plus to someone with a prohetic motivation. The prophet has to be *stubbornly* committed to bringing the Word of God no matter what opposition he may have to endure. A prophet is concerned with righting wrongs, exposing sin, and keeping God's reputation spotless. If your second or another child in the family is motivated in this way, you may find him a difficult child to live with. He will be correcting you, pointing out your errors, and trying to explain the correct way of doing things.

The motivation of prophet seems so alien to the personality of many passive, agreeable second-borns that you may think your child could not possibly have this gift. But remember, God gives us a gift that will strengthen our weaknesses. The second child doesn't like to be put into situations where he could be embarrassed, where he might have to withstand criticism, and where he will continually have to forgive. Yet this is often the position one with prophetic motivation must take.

Karl König says that the second child is "nearer to the Kingdom of God than any other person on earth. It is his prerogative, but it is also his danger. To be a second child mostly means to walk along a rope stretched between heaven and earth; to maintain the balance between above and below is the chief attribute of the second child."[15] Perhaps this accounts for that "schizophrenic" nature of the second child—trying to find his balance. As a second child myself, I found this statement interesting, especially since my last book was called *The Delicate Balance*. My whole life has been a search for balance and I have swung from one extreme to the other.

Perhaps if we parents could understand this concept we would be more effective with our second children. Armed with this information, we would not be surprised by their mood swings or extremes of behavior. We could stand ready to love them, accept them, discipline them, and direct them, confident that with our help and God's grace they will one day find that balance they are seeking.

Parenting Pointers

1. Do not put siblings in the same activity. It fosters unhealthy competition and comparison.

2. Be careful that your schedule is not always determined by the first-born. Allow the other children times when their activities are the most important.

3. See to it that your second baby gets plenty of verbal stimulation, especially in the first eighteen months of life.

4. Discover your second child's special area of creativity and encourage it.

5. Recognize his deep sensitivity to injustice and help him to understand that different treatment does not mean favoritism.

6. Use Scripture to reinforce your reason for rules. Encourage your second child to look up things in the Bible and understand God's reason for rules.

Ten

The Slighted
Middle Child

It has long been thought that it's better to be first or last, anything but the middle child in a family. Even those parents who know nothing about birth order will usually be familiar with the negative thinking surrounding the middle birth position. Before we can explore this position, we need to examine just who qualifies as a middle child. It is easy to discover the middle child in a family of three, especially when they are fairly closely spaced. But, how do you spot him in a larger family?

My first three children were each a year apart: boy, girl, boy. This established Shannon, my girl, as the middle child. The effects of the negative middle spot were softened somewhat, however, because she was the only girl, and therefore did have a special distinction. Four years later Kelly was born. Now, the number switched to four with two middle children. Shannon moved up the ladder to become the oldest girl and therefore her position was somewhat enhanced. Tom, however, the third-born, lost his distinctive role as the youngest child and became the more typical middle child.

There is no set formula for determining which child in a large family will be the most representative middle child. Richard Nixon, for instance, was a second child of four and may have remained a middle child except his older brother was frequently ill. Therefore the mantle of oldest child fell on his shoulders and he moved up a notch. The middle child may be the third child in a family of five. And I know a typical middle child who is the fourth in a family of nine. In a family of six children two would be middle children, but only one may show the characteristics we usually ascribe to a middle child.

As Bradford Wilson and George Edington, authors of *First Child, Second Child*, point out, position does not define a middle child so much as one particular trait:

> Far more important than any technical definition of "middlehood" is this type of subjective experience which characterizes it—the lifelong and never-ending search for belongingness. Because it is often the fate of your ordinal position to feel like a fifth wheel; an extra; a leftover who lives in dread of being completely bypassed and upstaged by elder and younger sibs—and anyone else in your environment.[1]

This is the true mark of a middle child—"a search for belongingness." It is easy to see why middle children may feel cheated. They are too young to reap the special advantages of the oldest child and too old to collect some of the goodies of the youngest. They are constantly being told, "You are too young to stay up as late as big brother" or "You are to old to act like such a baby."

Not surprisingly, then, researchers in surveying more than 2,000 middle-born teenage boys found being born in the middle tends to lower a youngster's self-esteem.[2] Prof. Jeannie S. Kidwell of the child and family studies department at the University of Tennessee's Knoxville campus explains this is because of "the 'lack of uniqueness' middle-borns suffer." She says they feel "cheated of parental attention and support and feel 'pushed around' by family rules and regulations." Also, those middle-borns spaced from brothers and sisters by about two years on either side showed the lowest self-esteem. Those either closer or farther apart tended to feel more positive about themselves.

Every child needs to feel a special role or place within the family. Frequently, the middle child cannot find that role so he moves outside the family to find his niche in life. The oldest and youngest children will have the deepest roots and needs within the family, while middle children may gain their feeling of uniqueness by belonging to a group, club, or gang outside the perimeters of the family. The middle child is more inclined, therefore, to accept the values of his peer group over and above the family value system since that is the group whose acceptance he is seeking.

Oddly when he rejects the family value system, he may also reject the rules and conventions that govern society and may become something of a noncomformist. So, although his life is a search to belong, he rejects the very rules that bring acceptance. Not only does he put himself outside the family circle but he also stands outside the rules of etiquette governing society, thumbing his nose at them, but desperately wanting acceptance by that society.

Some middle children respond to the challenge of finding a role in the family "by becoming verbally aggressive and developing an 'attention-getting' personality. One study shows they are the most 'changeable' of children, another that they are the least popular."[3] This may be because "the second of three is wedged in a situation which stimulates maximum competitive potential."[4] Also, this center birth position seems to affect girls more strongly than it affects boys. Dr. Lucille Forer says that "a middle boy among three boys usually is less anxious than either of his siblings, while the middle among three girls may be more serious, depressed, self-reproachful, and anxious than either of her sisters."[5] In fact, being the middle of three girls is the most difficult of all birth order positions because that girl has been found to be the least favorite child and the one the parents most wanted to be a boy.

Root of Bitterness

Probably the most difficult problem the middle child will encounter in life is in his relationships with others. If the family experience has not been positive, the same hurt and rejection felt in those relationships will be projected to other relationships. If, for instance, he suspects one of his friends has betrayed him, he can immediately terminate the relationship. My husband used to chide me about my ability to drop someone as if he never existed if I sensed rejection from him. Even though God has taught me much about forgiveness and tolerance, the most difficult experiences of my Christian life have involved other people and betrayal. The effects of my middle-child syndrome have continued to follow me into adulthood and even into my "new creature" Christianity.

This can lead to jealousy toward those they feel are more successful or have more material possessions, competitiveness, and an inability to maintain relationships. It is easy to see how all relationships will eventually become a reminder of the hurtful relationships of the family and the old jealousy will recur.

One sign that a middle child is having difficulty that mothers might become particularly aware of is a lack of gratefulness. Since the child grows up feeling cheated, he may feel subconsciously that every good thing that comes his way is due him to make up for the deficiency in his childhood. In his mind, God is just settling past unfair accounts.

But the most outstanding characteristic of an unhappy middle child is what the Bible calls a root of bitterness. Darlene was the third child of five and a typical middle child. I first became aware of her problem of bitterness when she began having relational conflicts with the three girls who were her roommates. The girls, members of our church, came to me in desperation because Darlene was making life miserable for all of them. I agreed to talk to her and tried to help her see all the good things God had done for her. She was a beautiful girl, athletically gifted, with a good education and a good job. I was amazed that she couldn't see anything positive about her life. Knowing she grew up overshadowed by a successful first-born sister and equally achieving second-born brother, I feared she never found her special place in the family and tried, unsuccessfully, to help her see it had affected her ability to find her place in the family of God as well. Since that time she has left our church home and moved on to several others, leaving in her wake unhappiness and strife.

Hebrews 12:15 talks about the results of this type of bitterness: "See to it that no one comes short of the grace of God; that no root of bitterness springing up causes trouble, and by it many be defiled" (NAS). In the fifteen years my husband and I have pastored a church, we have seen this root of bitterness in many people but most frequently in middle children. We have found that this is the most difficult spiritual problem to overcome because of the "many" it defiles.

This root of bitterness, which may be directed toward one parent, often will be a vague "floating hostility" that will then be directed toward other relationships as the child grows older. In this way the "many become defiled." It is difficult to pastor someone in whom bitterness has taken firm root because hostility toward his natural family will be directed toward those in authority in the spiritual family. He could carry this same "fifth wheel" feeling into Christianity, experiencing jealousy of those he feels are being favored by the spiritual parents.

I first saw this root of bitterness as a reality when praying with a woman named Carol a number of years ago. Several of us were praying with her for God to set her free from bitterness when she began to experience severe abdominal pain. She cried out for us to stop praying because, in her words, "it feels like a giant root is being pulled out of my stomach." We did stop and I began to study this root of bitterness mentioned in Hebrews 12.

It was not until five years later, during a three-day period of prayer and fasting in our church, that Carol called one morning, crying and asking for prayer once more. The previous night, her three closest friends had told her of some attitudes they had seen in her life that they felt were hurting their relationship with her. Carol told me later that she had been upset by their revelations but got on her knees before God and asked Him to show her if these things were true. She said that scene after scene of her early life began to replay itself in her head and she relived some very unhappy experiences. She was aware that the wrong attitudes her friends had mentioned were rooted in these experiences and her unforgiveness. She prayed forgiving her parents and brothers and sisters for each incident that God brought to her mind. It was four A.M. before she felt cleansed.

She called me that morning because she still felt the need of prayer. Several women and I went to her home and prayed asking God to remove that root of bitterness that had been so resistant five years before. During that time God's love had softened the soil around the root and Carol's forgiveness of her family broke its final hold on her life. She was totally set free that day and has walked in a new freedom with her brothers and sisters in the family of God since that time.

To be delivered from a root of bitterness the middle child must make it a practice to refuse the lies of rejection, to forgive others who are suspected of slighting him, and to express a thankful and praising heart. Parents could teach this child when young to focus on Scriptures such as Philippians 4:4, "Rejoice in the Lord always; again I will say, rejoice!" (NAS), and to study David's way of praising God in the Psalms. Parents can also play praise songs so there is an attitude of thanksgiving present in the home.

Ultimately, the middle child must also come to terms with his family and realize that it is not so much their rejection of him that is causing the problem but his rejection of them. Most of what he has interpreted as rejection was just an adolescent search for identity. To be healed of this root of bitterness it is necessary to forgive the family and parents in particular and to become vulnerable to them. A person who really wants a healing to take place will have to learn to trust his family once again. There is no better way for him to find his place in the family of God.

What can parents do to prevent their middle child or children from feeling this lack of uniqueness? The first thing is to be aware of the potential for this problem. If parents know that this is going to be the major problem in the life of their middle child they can take preparations to avoid it by helping the middle child find his special role. Perhaps it will be in some sports activity, maybe on the debating team (middle children are great debaters), or playing the snare drum in the marching band. What the child does is not as important as the fact that he is accomplishing something distinctive and unique. Also, since this child often gets lost in the shuffle between the aggressive first-born and the clinging youngest, parents need to take special time alone with him to make sure he has time to air his feelings and frustrations.

One middle child of our acquaintance who struggles with this root of bitterness complained the first time I ever met her that her parents had not allowed her to get braces. She came from a large family and money was always in short supply. For some reason, she focused on her slightly protruding front teeth and need for braces as the way her parents could prove their love for her. They hadn't and, in her mind, that was proof of their lack of concern. Her life has been a constant struggle for acceptance in relationships and much of this could have been prevented if her parents could have found some way to fulfill this desire.

So parents, be alert! Your middle child might focus your acceptance of her on some object or activity. Of course a new Mercedes is out of the question but if it seems to be a reasonable demand, and especially if it is something none of the other kids has received, it may be the very thing that proves your love for her.

Since many middle children may also be second- and third-born, all the parenting pointers for these two birth orders apply as well. The middle child carries that easily offended attitude of the second child, so it would be good to apply the lessons in forgiveness, keeping his mind disciplined against rejection. And like the third child, he has that lack of identity. The text of Jeremiah 29:11 would be a good life verse to teach the insecure middle child to give him a feeling of belonging, of being a special person with a special purpose in life: " 'For I know the plans that I have for you,' declares the Lord, 'plans for welfare and not for calamity to give you a future and a hope' "(NAS).

In spite of the disadvantages of being a middle child, most grow up to be well-adjusted and happy adults. Being in the middle has forced them to learn to relate to those older than themselves and to those who are younger and weaker. This produces children who are tactful and diplomatic. Lucille Forer says that because of this "the middle child may make his way in occupations where personal charm, ability to arbitrate, and the ability to manipulate rather than to take direct action involving others, are important characteristics. Politics, statesmanship, salesmanship are perhaps the kinds of occupations in which middle children might be found to attain superior status."[6]

Middle children are usually not as achievement-oriented as oldest and youngest children and the middle of three children seems to have the lowest need for intellectual achievement. But we know that highly achievement-oriented people are not necessarily happy people. Middle children have grown up in the midst of a family and have learned to relate to a number of people so they will be more successful than other children where human relations are important. They are also good "team" players since they have been used to cooperating with siblings. One extra plus for middle children in our divorce-prone society is that they are the most "monogamous" of all birth orders.[7]

Spiritual Gifts

The spiritual gift of the middle child will vary with the birth order. If the prevailing attitude in the life of the child is that of injustice, he may be prophetic in his gift like the second-born. Third children make good shepherds in the Body of Christ as we shall see in chapter twelve.

One spiritual gift that a middle child would function particularly well in is that of exhortation. An exhorter is one who is able to stimulate the faith of others. The middle child has learned to be tactful and diplomatic, so he has the ability to encourage each person in the way that is the most beneficial to his spiritual growth. Since the middle child is often discouraged and ungrateful, God can turn his weaknesses around and give him such zeal and thankfulness that he will be able to encourage others. The middle child is not accustomed to "center stage" like the oldest, only, and youngest, so he is able to stand behind someone and inspire him instead of worrying about his own advancement.

So, in spite of some real disadvantages to the middle birth position, there are some definite pluses. We middle children have a distinct advantage over other birth orders in learning how to make our weaknesses work for us. My greatest weakness as a middle child was that sense of not belonging. As a result, much of my life was a search for identity. When God apprehended me and brought me into His family, I knew I had found my identity; I knew I finally belonged. My sense of rootlessness was the very thing that brought me to find my roots in Jesus Christ. My weakness became God's strength (2 Corinthians 12:9). So help your middle child take heart—God has a special place for him or her in His family.

Parenting Pointers

1. Make sure middle children don't feel "lost" in the family structure but have a sense of belonging. This may be accom-

plished by responsibilities and special activities; and even nicknames bestow a certain honor.

2. Teach them to have a thankful and grateful heart. Have them memorize Scriptures and praise songs that pertain to these subjects.

3. Be sensitive to their real or imagined slights within the family and help them to learn to forgive.

4. Be aware that they may focus their acceptance on some object or activity. If within reason, try to provide that for them.

Eleven

The Search
for Identity

Many of the proponents of birth-order research recognize three different personalities: first, second, and third. The only child is a combination of first and third and the third child is equated with the youngest. Through personal observation and research over the years, however, I have come to the conclusion that the third child whether or not he is the youngest is a distinct personality type and can be quite different from a youngest child who may be fourth or fifth in the family. His is a complex personality and probably the most difficult for parents to understand. These next two chapters will focus on the third-born.

By the time the third child arrives, the first two children have established their rivalry and their approaches to gaining parental attention. Dr. James Bossard, in his study of one hundred large families, found that the third children, "finding these two roles pre-empted [responsible and agreeable], turn from the family to the community. They become social-minded and socially ambitious."[1]

Not only have the first two children preempted these roles in the family; Mom and Dad are usually not too worked up about the birth of baby number three. No wonder that Karl König calls the third child "an outsider" and the "lonely child."[2] He enters a world that pays minimal attention to his existence. Because he, like the middle child, finds no place in the family, he turns to the community and peers to find the acceptance he never feels within his family structure. If the third child is also a middle child, his problem will be further compounded by a root of bitterness and he may follow an independent path, rejecting all those he feels have rejected him. If the third child is also the youngest, he may capitalize on being the baby in order to secure special attention and services. If this method works for him and if he remains the baby long enough, he may choose to retain a dependent position throughout life. Whatever his response, though, all third children carry the pain of loneliness through their lives. They may appear happy and well-adjusted, or withdrawn and shy, but underneath both facades is a child who feels cut off from other people, who believes that no matter how hard he tries, he will never really fit in.

Satan, who always tries to capitalize on our weaknesses, attempts to reinforce the aloneness of the third child through the circumstances of life. The book *Breaking Points* is the story of John Hinckley, Jr., the young man who attempted to assassinate President Reagan. The story relates how John was born two days before the new hospital opened in the town of Ardmore, Texas. As a consequence, when he was transferred to the new hospital after it opened, he had to be kept in a room all by himself because of his exposure to the outside world. His mother, Jo Ann, in remembering the incident, felt this was symbolic. "Alone . . . separated from his peers . . . years later this was to become John's pattern."[3] From that moment of birth, Satan's lie to John was that he didn't fit in, that he was different. The tragedy is that John believed the lie and built his life on it.

The problems of my third child, Tom, were also rooted in a rejection that occurred even before his birth. During a routine gynecologic examination performed as a follow-up to major surgery, my doctor told me in an angry voice that I was three months pregnant. He went on to make dire predictions concerning the consequence of having another baby so soon after my operation. Since I didn't even know till that moment I was pregnant, I was stunned by the doctor's reaction. I remember going home that day and sobbing with fear. Although none of the doctor's predictions came true, the fear that was implanted in my mind led me to reject my child on the subconscious level from the moment I learned I was carrying him.

On the morning of Tom's birth I was the only patient in the labor room. My doctor was there, but he was more interested in having coffee with the nurses than in the progress of my labor. Consequently Tom entered the world without benefit of medical assistance. When a nurse grasped the situation, pandemonium broke loose. Three nurses, the obstetrician, and an anesthesiologist came running toward me and a nose cone was clapped over my face. The next thing I knew, I was waking up in the recovery room.

When I came to, I was in a little cubicle with my husband looking down at me, and our new baby was lying in an isolette next to me. With hardly a glance at the baby, I launched into a tirade about all the indignities I had suffered at the hands of my doctor and the entire hospital staff. When I paused for breath, my husband informed me that the baby was a boy. I had been so filled with resentment and self-pity that I hadn't even bothered to ask!

At the time of Tom's birth, I had given Satan a legal right to him by failing to accept and acknowledge him as my child. My self-centeredness had opened the door for a spirit of rejection to enter Tom. Today, we recognize the importance of bonding between the mother and the baby if the child is going to grow up secure in acceptance and love. I could not bond with Tom because I never had that moment of acceptance of him at birth. I didn't know then how important it is to hold your child and accept him right after birth, not only for the child's future security but also for protection from demonic forces that are looking for legal loopholes to attack our children. Because of my unconscious rejection of him, he was a whiny, unhappy child. This behavior caused me to further reject him and just compounded the problem.

My eyes might not have been opened if it had not been for the concern of Tom's fifth-grade teacher. She told me during a parent-teacher conference that Tom was becoming a behavior problem and she felt he was just trying to get attention. She said he was an underachiever and capable of much better work than he was producing.

As I began to pray earnestly for Tom, the Lord reminded me of the circumstances surrounding my pregnancy and Tom's birth. I saw how I had rejected Tom even before he was born. Because John and Shannon had established a good relationship, Tom never felt accepted by them either. Whenever he tried to break into their play time, John and he would start fighting and Shannon would just retreat to her room. I realized that Tom always seemed to stand on the perimeters of our family. Whenever there was a family fun time, Tom stood back a little from the rest of us, watching, but not really joining in. Even his younger sister, Kelly, who became Tom's playmate, could not draw him into the family.

As I sat there remembering that morning, it all seemed so clear; I couldn't believe I hadn't realized it before. I began to cry for the hurt and rejection Tom must have felt all those years. I thanked God for His promise in Joel 2:25: "I will make up to you for the years That the swarming locust has eaten . . ." (NAS). Since "Jesus Christ is the same yesterday and today, yes and forever" (Hebrews, 13:8, NAS) we are not bound by time. We can undo the things that happened years ago as if they never were.

I remembered that scene in the nursery eleven years before, but this time I looked at my son and accepted him fully as my child. I prayed out loud, "Satan, I take back all the legal claim I gave you to my son Tom in this instance. I accept him fully as my son." I prayed this same prayer many times as the Holy Spirit brought to mind all the situations when I conveyed to my son this attitude of rejection. After many such affirmations, the day came when I began to say, "I accept him fully as my son"—but I couldn't speak. Tears rolled down my cheeks and I began to sob. In that moment, I knew that my acceptance of Tom was complete, that Satan's hold on him was broken.

Over the years, Tom had accepted many lies that the enemy had whispered such as: "Your mother doesn't really love you" and "You don't really belong in this family." Even though he had a long fight ahead of him, the ultimate victory belonged to Jesus, who gives us power over the enemy. It took eleven years for Tom to believe the lies about himself and it would take God eight years to bring him into total freedom—a battle at a time.

I believe Satan's major hold over each of our lives is through a lie that begins when we are very young, or like Tom, even in the womb. The lie may be that we are not wanted, that we are stupid and will never do well in life, or even that we are evil. Whatever the lie, though, Satan reinforces it through life's circumstances. As we mentally accept the lie, we give it (and Satan) power over us to bring the lie into reality. The first step is breaking the central lie. Then we have to learn to "be transformed by the renewal of your mind" (Romans 12:2, ML). The lie can be broken by a sixty-second prayer but the renewing of our mind will take a long time. As our thoughts line up with God's thoughts about us, we will begin to understand "what is the good and acceptable will of God" for our lives. As parents, we can pray for the wisdom to see the lies Satan has implanted in each of our children's lives, release them from the lies, and then teach them to renew their minds through the Word of God.

Thus, isolation or separation becomes the deepest problem for the third child. Karl König says that "they feel apart, sometimes even cut off from all other people. . . . It bears the sting of inferiority. The child longs to take its place among other people, yet it lives under the firm impression that the others are not concerned with its existence and do not care to make its acquaintance."[4] He is quick to add that although many people suffer from feelings of inferiority from time to time, with the third child, "it is the fundamental layer of its social behavior." He is a part of the family circle, yet he is not; he longs to be one of the others, but he can never achieve this goal. Since he can't find his identity within the family circle, his life becomes a search for identity outside. This is why many third children drift through life aimlessly, classic underachievers, until they find a goal. Then there is often an immediate turn around in their behavior.

Many third-borns, like John Hinckley and my son Tom, accept the role of black sheep in their search for identity. They would rather have the distinction of an undesirable trait than not to have any identity at all.

Just recently there was an article in the *Chicago Tribune* Magazine Section on a woman body-builder, Jo Wood.[5] She was the third and youngest of three girls. Her mother and father were achievers and her two older sisters both have multiple advanced degrees. In her own words, her two older sisters "knew where they were going. From adolescence on, they did everything right." Jo, on the other hand, said she "was a little misfit." She drifted aimlessly through school and several colleges "still in search of everything her family had found years before." The turning point came the day she walked into the school weight room and realized she could become the strongest woman in the world. At that moment Jo Wood found her identity, as unusual as it might seem to most women. Since that time she has put her life in danger through the misuse of drugs and severe training techniques. She is willing to risk even her life to keep her sense of identity—the pain of training is nothing compared to the pain of isolation.

The Root of the Problem

There is an amazing story in the first chapter of the book of Hosea. Hosea, a prophet of God, was commanded to marry an unfaithful wife and conceive children with her. This was to symbolize the unfaithfulness of the children of Israel "in departing from the Lord." Each of the three children born to Gomer and Hosea was given a symbolic name and this symbolism has amazing accuracy in the lives of the first three children.

The first child born was a son. "Then the Lord said to Hosea, 'Call him Jezreel, because I will soon punish the house of Jehu for the massacre at Jezreel, and I will put an end to the kingdom of Israel' " (verse 4, NIV). *The Expositor's Bible Commentary* states: "The use of the name Jezreel here looks *back to the time and also ahead to a future day*, when 'the blood' Jehu then shed would be avenged, as the next words indicate"[6] (italics mine). This is the very characteristic of the first child: "He has two faces—one is turned to his parents who represent the past; the other looks on to his brothers and sisters, thereby gazing into the future."[7]

The second child born was a daughter. "Then the Lord said to Hosea, 'Call her Lo-Ruhamah, for I will no longer show love to the house of Israel, that I should at all forgive them' " (verse 6). Her name means literally, "Not loved." In chapter eight, I discussed the fact that the deepest problem of second children is rejection—a feeling of not being loved.

Finally, Gomer had a third child, a son. "Then the Lord said, 'Call him Lo-Ammi, for you are not my people, and I am not your God' (verse 9). The name Lo-Ammi is harsher in meaning than the name of the second child. The name Lo-Ruhamah spoke of not being loved; Lo-Ammi speaks of being fully disowned."[8] This is precisely the problem of every third child—feeling disowned from his family, not a part.

Al was a young man who joined our fellowship about eight years ago when he was engaged to a woman in our church. He was the third and youngest of three boys and though he was a likeable young man, he appeared to be without any drive or ambition. After his marriage, he drifted from job to job, finding something wrong with the boss, conditions on the job, always something. His spiritual life was in the same condition. Although he had made a commitment to Jesus Christ, he never seemed to grow and change. It was frustrating for my husband and me who, as leaders, could see the great gifts and potential in Al but were helpless to know how to unlock them.

Al had been a Christian seven years when we had our usual mid-winter retreat for the whole fellowship. We invited a man called Ian Andrews from England with a gift of healing. Ian spoke on what he called the "orphan spirit" and said that many Christians don't really feel that God is their Father because of this. Al readily identified with this problem but received no personal ministry on the retreat. He continued, however, to pray and seek God's help.

Several weeks later as he was driving home from work, he heard that still small voice of God asking him if he was tired of the way he was. Al replied that yes, he was sick of himself and desired to change. God then indicated to him that he needed to give all of his heart to Him. Al pictured himself giving his heart to God and with that came a release from the sense of abandonment and in its place a spirit of adoption from God.

The change in Al has been miraculous. In the year-and-a-half since being set free, he has entered fully into the things of God. He has emerged as a leader in the church, teaching and praying for many who have received healing. He has also settled down to one job and has proved a faithful and valuable employee. Where he once felt that he was not a part of the Body of Christ—that it was just an extension of his family life—now he feels an intimate part of the fellowship. The change came about because he finally found an identity—not just a worldly identity, rather his identity in Jesus Christ.

Because the third child has felt isolated from people, he has a hard time trusting. Since he never gives his heart fully to anyone, he also has a hard time giving his whole heart to God. So many, like Al, limit themselves from coming into their full potential because God cannot bring us into His plan for our lives if we are not willing to trust Him with our whole heart. After this experience, a particular Scripture, Galatians 4:4–6, became a reality to Al.

> But when the fulness of time came, God sent forth His Son, born of a woman, born under the Law, in order that He might redeem those who were under the Law, that we might receive the *adoption as sons*. And because you are sons, God has sent forth the Spirit of His Son into our hearts, crying, "Abba! Father!" (NAS, italics mine)

If parents realize that the third-born's greatest problem is a lack of identity, we can begin early to help alleviate the problem. All children need to know that they are special persons in the Kingdom of God. (This feeling, by the way, is something that first children almost always possess.) They need to have a special sense of destiny as a motivating force in their lives. Every Christian mother should point out to all her children—but particularly to child number three—the unique gifts they possess and the ways in which God will be able to use them for His glory.

Tom first made a commitment to the Lord when he was eight years old. For about four years he had a deep interest in the spiritual side of life. During this time we talked many times about the "call" God had on his life. He felt that he would be in some type of full-time service for the Lord someday. I used those talks as an opportunity to reinforce that sense of purpose or destiny for his life. During his years of wandering away from God, he said he always remembered that feeling of a destiny in God and that was probably the thing that kept him from "going over the edge."

God has a plan for every life. We need to pray for wisdom to know how to guide each one of our children in the direction that God has chosen for them. God would not give us authority over our children without giving us the wisdom to direct their lives. That third child needs special encouragement and love to find God's path for his life. God can help us meet this need in our third child and see that his life will not be an empty search for identity.

In this chapter I have identified the major problem of the third child. In the next chapter we will look at some practical ways parents can help this child find God's plan for his life.

Parenting Pointers

1. Recognize that your third child's greatest problem will be a feeling of isolation or abandonment.

2. Pray for the wisdom to recognize the lies Satan has implanted in your third-born's mind and pray to break them.

3. Make sure your third child has a special sense of destiny in the Kingdom of God.

Twelve

Parenting the Third Child

Because third children feel alienated from the family circle, neglected and rejected, they often have a lot of distrust toward other people. Dr. König found that, because of this, they "either *withdraw into their own being* and build a fence or even a wall against the hostile world, or they gather their strength together and after having done so, break out and *try to conquer by force* that which otherwise would not yield to them"[1] (italics mine).

Withdrawal

We have seen that the first child's goal in life is to lead. The second wants to live in harmony with the world and therefore resists change. The third often responds to conflict by withdrawing and has a tendency to be a "peace at any price" person.

146

Third-borns try to escape a direct meeting with the world and live beyond reality. Because they lack a strong sense of identity and purpose, they tend to turn away from an obstacle rather than try to overcome it. This is why they are so often the underachievers in the classroom.

It would be wise for parents to keep a close check on their third-born's classroom progress and attitude by occasional visits to his teacher. Does he complete homework assignments? Is he attentive? Does he participate in class discussions? Is he working up to his ability? Check these questions with his teacher. In this way you could anticipate future problems in school and take proper steps to correct them. I have found that teachers are more than willing to cooperate with a parent when it has to do with improvement of class attitude and performance of a student. If the parents don't defend their child but submit to the teacher's suggestions and ensure their cooperation, they will have a strong ally.

When Tom was in the eighth grade, he decided to run for class president. He was excited about the campaign, making posters and passing out buttons, but when he made it into the finals, he found out he would have to give a speech in front of the whole school. As I helped him the evening before with his speech, I could see the fear and desire to escape in his eyes. This was something he hadn't bargained for.

The next morning he was quite nauseated and told me he couldn't possibly go to school. My heart went out to him because I knew he really felt sick, but I realized I couldn't let him retreat. As gently as I could I told him he had to go and make his speech because, as I explained to him, "If you run from this, you'll be running the rest of your life. Everything that is too difficult, you will not attempt." I assured him I would be praying for him and almost pushed him out the door closing my ears to his pleas to stay home. He did get through the speech and, even though he wasn't elected president, he won a major victory.

In his junior year of high school, he joined the soccer team.

He soon found the daily training sessions, run by a competitive coach, a grueling experience. He told me that every morning as he pedaled his bike to practice, he would begin to feel his stomach tighten as he thought of trying to keep up with the other players. Finally, about halfway through summer training, he once again wanted to drop out. I reminded him that he could not run from this either, and encouraged him to remain and finish out the season. He decided he would and even stayed on the team his senior year.

If we can help our children understand that God's purpose in the classroom, at home, and even in sports activities is character development rather than achievement, it will make it easier to "hang in there" when the going gets tough. In this way our children will have a sense of accomplishment just from doing their best and staying with it regardless of whether they are the A+ students or the team heroes. We told Tom as he sweated his way through two seasons of soccer, "God is more interested in the steadfastness and reliability you are developing through soccer than whether you win or lose or are the star player."

The third-born will need more encouragement than other children. Perhaps giving him a special job or function, or asking him to tell Aunt Mary about some event at school, or giving him responsibility for family chores will help to make him feel a useful part of the family.

Moses is the best biblical illustration of a third-born and displays the tendency to run or withdraw from conflict—after the murder of the Egyptian (Exodus 2:11–15) and also in his encounter with God at the burning bush (Exodus 3:11; 4:1,13). Yet God did use this weakness of Moses as a strength. When his leadership was threatened by his sister, Miriam, and his brother, Aaron (Numbers 12:1–2), by the people (Numbers 14:1–4; 16:41–42), and by Korah and the 250 leaders of the congregation (Numbers 16:1–3), Moses refused to confront them and defend himself. Instead he turned to God for his defense and in each instance God Himself reaffirmed Moses' leadership. We can also help our third child by using the life of Moses to show him how God can transform our weakness into His strength. If, when our third child feels like running from a situation, he can turn to God instead, then he will not only be able to overcome any obstacle but he will be finding his identity in God.

Humor

If the third child tries to "conquer by force," the force most often used is humor. Since the third child sits back on the fringes of the family or peer group, he becomes an excellent observer of people. The first child, who is usually in the center of whatever is happening, has the least discernment of people and understanding of human relationships. The third child, however, has a tremendous understanding of the foibles of human nature and often uses this wisdom in a humorous approach to life. Dr. Lillian Canzler has made a specialty of finding out what makes children between five and eight years old laugh. She says that children use humor "as a sort of power control."[2] Adults also use humor to control group behavior but in a more sophisticated manner. Often the third-born's claim to fame in the family is the ability to make the others laugh.

Not only do third children use humor to control situations but they use it as a defense to avoid disclosing their own thoughts or feelings of uneasiness or discomfort. The third-born's distrust of people keeps him from sharing his emotions with those around him. The description of Jenny, a third child in the novel *Dinner at the Homesick Restaurant*, might well be a description of all third-borns: ". . . Jenny was so brisk and breezy but . . . oh, you might say somewhat opaque, a reflecting surface flashing your own self back at you, giving no hint of her self."[3]

Third children are the most emotionally immature in the family constellation. Maturity comes from relationships and this is the very thing that the third child misses out on in the family. We must be careful not to let our third children hide behind a mask of family comedian or to assume that because the child seems happy and optimistic on the surface, all is well beneath the surface. Tom was my happiest and, I thought, best-adjusted teenager. I had no idea what was bubbling underneath that façade until after his deliverance from drugs when he showed me his journals. Page after page was filled with cries for help, thoughts of suicide, and pessimistic ponderings on the state of the world. I had been fooled by that outer façade of optimism and had not taken the time to search beneath the surface and help Tom deal with the maelstrom of emotions.

If we do not take the time to help our children understand and deal with their emotions, they will become shallow, underdeveloped adults who either make a joke of every uncomfortable situation or else withdraw completely. It is not easy to draw a third child out emotionally because most of them feel like a friend of mine who said that no one in her family ever asked her what she was thinking or feeling. As a result, she learned to keep her thoughts and feelings to herself. In doing this, though, the child never experiences the objective counsel of others who are more experienced and who can help him deal objectively rather than subjectively with his thoughts and feelings. Parents need to take the time to talk to him in a slow, unhurried setting, which will allow the third child plenty of time to share what he is really feeling. It would be a good idea to spend some time alone each week with this child so that he does not have to compete with brothers and sisters for attention. Once he is convinced that we really are interested in him, it will be easy to win his trust and help him to share his feelings.

A good exercise for third children would be to have them keep a daily journal. Encourage them to write down their thoughts and feelings. In this way they don't have to deal with face-to-face encounters that might make them uneasy and keep them from sharing at a deep level. The beginning efforts at a journal may be awkward since third children are not used to sharing deep thoughts and feelings but encourage them to keep at it and in a short time they will be amazed at the freedom they will have in writing.

Fantasy

Sharon Wegscheider-Cruse, author of *Another Chance*, a guide for professionals who work with alcoholics, has found interesting information about the third child. She calls him "The Lost Child" because he doesn't try for attention the way the first and second children do. He stays out of everyone's way and avoids the family chaos. Although this is accentuated by the alcoholic family, it is the same role every third child adopts. She further states:

> In a family where communication among all the members is poor, he is the most out of touch. . . . Interest in his undertakings, praise for his achievements, reassurance in his fears, companionship and affection in his loneliness—none of these necessities of childhood is forthcoming from those who would normally provide them. Because he is so often out of sight, he and his needs are also out of mind.
>
> As the child retreats behind his wall of isolation, *he often builds a fantasy world of his own*, where for a few years he seems to find peace and satisfaction. So he spends a lot of time in his room, playing, reading, pursuing a hobby, or just daydreaming.
>
> But he cannot remain in his private little world forever. . . . He has had little experience in either expressing his own feelings or handling such expressions from others; in cooperation or in negotiating disputes. . . . He has had little experience in living. In his confusion he makes many errors in judgment with results that range from ineffectiveness to downright humiliation[4] (italics mine).

The third child's separation and lack of identity within the family may cause him to "build a fantasy world" for himself. Because he is not pushed to talk early as are the older children, he has plenty of time for the pictorial and imaginative thinking that characterizes mental activity before children acquire speech. This is why later-born children are more creative than their older brothers and sisters. Big brother and sister are not allowed the time to daydream and imagine—they must be about their father's business.

Adding to this tendency to fantasize is another special feature of the third child's character: He is a person of the future, a visionary.[5] Because of this, the "discrepancy between ideal and reality is a deep-seated quality in third children."[6] Other children are aware, especially as they grow older, of the difference between fantasy and reality. The third child cannot easily tell the difference. In an extreme case like that of John Hinckley, both blend together in a bizarre way. Since John had no identity of his own, he took the identity of a movie character who attempted to assassinate a president and then lived out that role in real life. John's father recognized this tendency in John's life: "A lack of realism. That's what concerned me about John as he reached senior high school, lack of any concept of what it took to get ahead in the real world."[7]

Recognizing this tendency to fantasize, we need to carefully monitor our third-born's intake of fantasy. Movies, television, plays, books, and especially rock music will have a profound effect on his life. Another child may be able to separate the real from the fabrication, but not the third-born. We should not allow him to spend hours watching TV or reading and listening to music alone in his room. See to it that he is involved in after-school activities that will keep his mind in the real world.

One of the greatest contributing factors to Tom's drug problem was his deep interest in rock music. The other children had the normal adolescent interest in this music of their peers but Tom was involved with it. Songs are a powerful tool for good or evil because they not only reach our minds through the words but also our spirits through the music. Tom seemed to enter into the fantasy world of the rock musician and he was tremendously influenced to follow that lifestyle. The first thing he did after God delivered him from drugs was to get rid of all the rock music that had seduced him away from God.

One of the greatest challenges to the parents of third children is to help them blend together the gap between their ideal world and the reality of everyday life. I have heard many adult third-borns confess to a search for the "big dream." They function in their daily jobs but never give themselves totally because someday they believe they are going to find that perfect fantasy job that will completely fulfill all their dreams. They are easily bored by detailed and repetitive chores but this is the very thing needed to bring reality into the third-born's life—the realization and acceptance that much of life is boring and drudgery but that this, too, is necessary.

The tendency to fantasize may explain another weakness of the third child: the propensity to lie. Dr. Haim Ginott, author of *Between Parent and Child,* says that children often lie "to give themselves in fantasy what they lack in reality. Lies tell truths about fears and hopes. They reveal what one would like to be or to do."[8] He encourages parents to use the information gained from a lie to help the child distinguish between reality and wishful thinking. If your third child tells you that he saw a monster in his room, rather than telling him he is lying, try to find out the fear that is the basis of his fantasy. If a child says that he got a monkey for Christmas, it would be better to reply, "You wish you had a monkey," rather than tell him he is lying. In this way you can help him distinguish between the real and the imaginary.

The first child is a child of the past. His function is to carry the past into the present. The second child is a child of the present—today is what matters. The third child lives in the future and has a hard time functioning in the reality of today. These are the students who are always daydreaming in class or doodling in their notebooks instead of taking notes. Their bodies are living in the here and now but their minds are somewhere in the future. They drive parents (especially first-born parents) and teachers to distraction. They are the underachievers, the dreamers, designers of the future, and the "Lost Child" in America—the nation of the first-borns.

In our country, it is the first-borns or the aggressive doers who are rewarded. They perform better in school and, since many jobs are tied into the educational system, the first-borns have the edge. Even though my third child had the same IQ level as his first-born brother, their grades were markedly different. John was a straight A student; Tom was satisfied with C's. Even if a third child develops an ambitious attitude to gain his parents' (especially father's) approval, he is going against his inner nature and will eventually have problems.

What are we to do with these dreamers then? Do we just let them drift through life without ever achieving anything substantial? One thing we find with third children that contributes to the pattern of underachieving is the lack of pressure brought on them by their parents. First children get the full brunt of parental pressure and expectations and the second may get the residual spilloff, but third children are left to drift through life at their own pace. All the third children I interviewed mentioned an absence of pressure. On the surface this would seem to be a good thing but it is conveying to the child a lack of interest, a feeling that the child is not as capable as child number one. The findings of University of Tennessee researchers showed that pressure to achieve had a positive effect on a child's self-esteem.[9] So, by not pressuring our third children to achieve, we are, in effect, saying, "You are not capable of achieving; therefore, I am not going to waste my time with you." Remember, without pressure there is no growth.

All of those third-borns also said that they found acceptance if they did average work so they didn't bother to push themselves, and this became the pattern for their lives, even for their Christian lives. We need to know our children's capabilities and then set expectations for them. Our expectations have to be realistic and we must be willing to spend time working with the child to help him attain those expectations. This is telling our third child,

"You are capable of doing much better and because I love you I will take the time to work with you to see you fulfill those expectations."

A child will respond to the way he is treated. If he is treated as the "spacey" one, as many third children are, he will develop that personality. It requires a lot of energy to keep a third child motivated, but is well worth the effort. It is also good to help third children set and reach goals because they are idealistic rather than realistic, and they often set unrealistically high goals for themselves, thereby dooming themselves to failure. The first child is a self-motivator. The second, unless discouraged, will be motivated by the goal of surpassing the first-born. But the third child sees no readily obtainable goals. We can help our third child by setting reachable, short-term goals that they can achieve, thereby giving them a feeling of success.

Probably what helped my third-born sister, Jeannie, to achieve success in life was her desire to be a nurse. From the time she was about five years old this became her goal in life. We never did know what implanted that desire in her mind, but she never swayed from it. Although she was a typical third-born underachiever, my parents used the goal of nursing to keep her motivated. In high school she knew if she didn't study for her science classes and get good grades, she wouldn't be able to handle the more difficult science classes in nursing school. Having a long range career goal helped her accomplish the short-term goals and kept her motivated. Although she hated studying and didn't enjoy one minute of her classroom time in nursing, she lived for her time in the hospital. It was the people and their care that drew her, not the scholastic end.

My third-born husband, John, also suffered through his four years of dental school. He disliked the classes but enjoyed his experience in the clinic with patients. He was, in turn, able to encourage our son Tom when he was struggling through his college years. Our third-borns need to know that they are not usually going to enjoy school and the reality of daily discipline but that it is a necessary "evil" in their lives to achieve their long-term goals or to bring their visionary dreams into reality.

The Spiritual Ones

Dr. Phillip Very, professor of psychology at Rhode Island College, believes that third children are the most spiritual ones in the family. As the basis for his theory he uses Seth, the third-born son of Adam. He was born to Adam in his old age "and is, therefore, 'the gift of God.' Hence his spirituality."[10] He also relates that in Christian Europe, it was traditional for the eldest son to inherit the family lands, for the second son to become a merchant or banker dealing with the public, and for the third son to enter the priesthood.

It is interesting that the Old Testament priesthood line was chosen from the descendants of Levi, the *third* son of Jacob (Numbers 3). This line supplied the priests, temple attendants, and teachers. Third children are usually underrepresented in church leadership but this may be due to their shy, withdrawn nature rather than a lack of spirituality. Third children will not push themselves into leadership but remain on the fringes waiting to be asked. Even then, though, they are often reluctant, as Moses was, to assume spiritual leadership.

We have found in our church that it is the third-borns who make the best "shepherds" or house group leaders. There are plenty who want to be leaders within the church, many for the wrong reasons, such as control. The third child knows what it is like to be a sheep without a shepherd because that is precisely the way he felt growing up. Jesus' concern was not for church buildings, programs, choir robes, or the number of people at weekly worship, but for the people themselves. "And seeing the multitudes, He felt compassion for them, because they were distressed and downcast like sheep without a shepherd" (Matthew 9:36, NAS). Third-borns are concerned about people and will take the time to listen and encourage. Just as the temple priests interceded for the people and went before God with their needs, so the third-born shepherd excels at interceding for the needs of the people.

A shepherd may be a man or a woman; the qualifying factor is a deep need and love for others. Many women with this gift take younger Christian women under their wing to discipline them both in practical and spiritual ways. When I think of the women in our church who function the most in the gift of hospitality, it is third-born women. This is their way of shepherding.

One other characteristic that makes third-borns good shepherds is that they are idealistic. Because of this, they see people not as they are today, but as they will be in God. I have often been amazed at my third-born husband's gift to overlook the problems in a man or woman and rather encourage him or her to become the person God had in mind when He created him or her. I usually can't see beyond the problem and become frustrated because I don't see the growth I think should be taking place.

Because the third child has this deep need for the spiritual side of life, we must help direct him to a relationship with God. Don't be put off by the façade the third child has erected with humor or withdrawal or moodiness. Beneath that exterior is a heart that has a deep desire to know and walk with God. You could do a Bible study with your third-born on self-worth and encourage him to ask God for some specific verses for his life. Make sure you write these verses down and remind him occasionally of them.

The first-born's danger is that he will try to work his way to God; the second is often too caught up in enjoying himself to think about his future with God; but the stumblingblock for the third is the feeling that God, like his siblings and parents, is not really interested in him and has no special plan for his life. If we can convince our third children that God truly does love them and has a special plan for their lives, we will help them avoid the pitfalls of low self-esteem and aimlessness that mark the lives of so many third children.

Parenting Pointers

1. Do not let your third child withdraw from conflict. Instead teach him to talk out or write out what he is feeling. Never let him stay home from school to avoid a test or other difficult situation.

2. Carefully monitor his schoolwork and keep in touch with the teacher so that you are aware of underachievement.

3. Give him a special responsibility with the family so that he will feel an integral part.

4. Beware of your third-born using humor to control or cover over his feelings in a situation.

5. Have him keep a journal.

6. Carefully monitor his intake of fantasy through television, radio, books, and movies. Give him detail work to do to help him focus on reality. See that he is involved in group activities after school.

7. Know his capabilities and keep the pressure on him to achieve at his level. Be willing to spend time working with him and take away a special privilege if he does not study.

8. Spend time teaching him that God has a special plan for his life. Do a Bible study on self-worth.

Thirteen

The
Overprotected Child

From the moment of his birth into this world, a baby strives to connect himself with his mother. We call the connecting process *bonding* and although we still do not understand the full impact of this mysterious development, we now know that it is vital to the future well-being of the child.

It is the mother who gives the child his first contact with another human being. Adler says that the mother is the child's "first bridge to social life; and a baby who could make no connection at all with his mother, or with some other human being who took her place, would inevitably perish."[1] For this reason, many hospital nurseries employ women whose sole job is to hold and love the newborn infants who lose their mothers. They know from past experience that a baby, even though given total health care, will die if not held and loved.

The mother should be a bridge and not a barrier. It is her job first to connect the child to herself and then extend that connection to the father, other children in the family, and eventually the whole social world around her.

The mother usually bonds closely to her first child and this could be a drawback to the child's interest in other people. The birth of the second child, though, pushes the first child toward the father and in this way enlarges the child's world. With the birth of each succeeding baby, the present one is pushed away from the mother toward the father and other siblings. In fact, "the effect of being dispossessed by a later-born child seems to be the development of more independence."[2] The youngest, however, has no successors, no one to push him away from mother's protective arms. For this reason, the youngest child often has the strongest bonding to the mother and, therefore, is the most dependent.

The mother, knowing this is her last child, her final chance to prove her worth as a mother, often clings to this terminal baby in a way that she hasn't with any other child. Then, too, there is the ever-present question, "Why *was* this child last?" Often the last child is an accident—the caboose baby—or the mother's attempt to rekindle a burned-out marriage. This youngest child may be born with a physical handicap and the parents decide to have no more children. Researchers found that "among children with congenital defect, there were significantly more last borns than first borns."[3] For these and other reasons, parents may have guilt because of their feelings toward the child and, in an attempt to deny these feelings, may spoil and overprotect this last child. (The overprotected child is not always the youngest. He may be a handicapped child, an only girl in the middle of all boys, or a fragile or sensitive child that the mother feels needs to be protected.) What effect does this pampering have on the child? Fear is often one of the strongest results.

Fear

Because of the strong bonding with the mother, the youngest child is often "tied to her apron strings." As long as the child can stay close to Mother, all is well. When the child feels that the mother is not as attentive as she ought to be, he soon learns that the quickest way to have her constant attention is by means of fear. Adler says that "all pampered children suffer from fear."[4] This is the way they keep their connection with the mother and so they build it into their way of life. The youngest child may show many fears such as fear of the dark, sleeping alone, or being left with a baby-sitter. All these fears are an attempt to keep the mother to himself.

My youngest child, Kelly, was the only one of our four children whom we allowed to sleep in our bed at times. She would use any excuse to try to get into our room. During the night, if we had a thunderstorm, she would be in our bed at the first crackle outside. Since she was our "baby" we indulged her. Then she began to find other excuses to want to sleep with us. Finally we realized a serious problem was developing and began to be firm with her about sleeping in her own bed.

Paul, in his letter to the Hebrews, says, "Let marriage be held in honor among all, and let the marriage bed be undefiled . . ." (Hebrews 13:4). Although Paul is specifically referring to the sins of adultery and fornication, allowing our children to sleep with us night after night is also "defiling the marriage bed." God intends that the unity of husband and wife be impenetrable and complete. If we allow our children to share our bed, they will soon become a wedge in the unity of the marriage. Probably disagreements over the care and discipline of children do more to injure a marriage than any other source except finances. We need to keep our marriage bed "undefiled" and a private place reserved for the husband and wife. The child may fight initially to stay in his parents' bed, but will eventually submit if he senses unity between husband and wife.

Illness is also a safe refuge for a pampered child and is related to fear. It is another ploy to keep Mother's attention focused on him. Although Kelly was excited about starting school, she often had stomachaches in the morning and would have stayed home if I had allowed it. Because I had struggled with fear-induced illness myself, I recognized this tendency in Kelly and would not let her stay home from school unless she was really ill.

The overprotected child is often plagued by a predisposition to sickness and will never overcome it till he deals with the fear he feels.

Many youngest children use their position of weakness as an advantage. I can remember Kelly crying because she always lost the board games to the older children. I would usually take them aside and exhort them to "let her win once in a while." Also, youngest children often resort to screaming and tattling on the older children to enlist Mom's help. Frequently, while in the kitchen preparing dinner, I would hear Kelly yelling from the family room that someone hit her or stole her toy. Without even going in to check on what was really taking place, I would automatically yell at the other children, usually my oldest, to stop annoying her. If the truth had been known, it was usually Kelly who had annoyed the others to the point of complete frustration. When they acted out their frustration, she screamed for and got my assistance.

This response, however, only teaches our children to be manipulative. Often mothers are manipulated by guilt into doing something for the last-born without even realizing it. Psychologist Rudolf Dreikurs says the youngest has to use a whole bagful of tricks to mask his situation as the smallest of the family, and, as a result, becomes quite inventive and adroit.[5]

One afternoon just as I was finishing a counseling session, Kelly burst through the door from school. She immediately came into the living room and began telling me an incident that occurred at school. I asked her if she would wait a few minutes as the woman was just leaving. With that, Kelly left the room mumbling that I never had time for her. I started to feel guilty until I realized that none of what she was mumbling was true. I gave Kelly more time and attention then I had given any of my other children. After the woman left I told Kelly that I did not accept her accusations since they were not true and I would not let her manipulate me into feeling guilty. Even though she was only in the fifth grade, the guilty smile she got on her face told me she knew perfectly well what she was doing.

Youngest children, even as adults, probably manipulate through guilt more than any other birth-order position. Oldest children are usually outwardly manipulative but the baby can get you to do what he wants by devious means. We need to recognize this tendency in our youngest children and not allow them to get away with it in childhood or they will grow up to be manipulative adults. Occasionally, even in adult relationships, I have had to fight the guilt projected on me by women friends. When I recognize this, it is usually a woman who was a youngest child.

It has been found that the "youngest child remains the disciplinary responsibility of the mother" even though Father may have disciplined all the other children.[6] In this way the mother keeps the youngest to herself and protects him from the father. When Kelly was in high school my husband often accused me of protecting her from him. I had to admit this was true and made a conscious effort to turn the responsibility of discipline over to him. I also found myself defending her to the other children even when she was obviously in the wrong. If the mother continues to defend her youngest, he may become a chronic coward always hiding behind her.

Mothers need to see that allowing a child to use fear or weakness as an advantage will reinforce the child's need to remain weak and helpless. If we want our youngest to grow up strong and responsible then we are going to have to stop fighting his battles for him and stop being manipulated by him. We will have to protect our younger children from undue teasing and domination by older siblings, but not go overboard and protect them from ever growing up.

Learning to Release

Mothers need to release all their children but especially this last child because the bond is so strong. I became aware of the strong need to sever the umbilical cord that binds them to us through an incident in my son Tom's life. As part of his training in Youth With A Mission, Tom went to Paris for a term. As we walked away from him at the airport, I mentioned to his sister Kelly that he still looked like a little boy living in a fantasy world. Several nights later we received a long-distance telephone call from Tom. He said he was feeling unbelievable fear and anxiety and wanted to come home. His father wisely suggested that he stay a few days and not make any snap decisions. Tom agreed and said he would call back in a few days.

The next night I was awakened about one A.M. by another phone call from Paris. Tom said that he was still not feeling any better about his situation and what did I think he should do. His father was out of town so I told Tom I would trust him to seek the Lord and discern His will. When I hung up the phone, I began praying for Tom. All of a sudden I heard myself praying, "I cut the umbilical cord that binds Tom to me and release him to You, Lord." After that I rolled over and fell asleep.

The next morning I realized I had no anxiety or concern about Tom but knew he was truly released to God. Thinking about the way the Holy Spirit had led me to cut the umbilical cord, I realized that Tom had been my "baby" for four years until his sister was born and, because he was the younger boy, I had retained somewhat of a protective attitude toward him. I would even teasingly call him my "baby boy." About mid-morning I received another phone call from Tom but this time it was a different Tom who was speaking. Gone were the fear and anxiety that had been so evident in his earlier calls.

"Well, I've made my decision," were Tom's first words. "I'm going to come home, and the strangest thing has happened to me." Tom then went on to tell me that a real peace had come over him about the time of my prayer the previous night, which was nine A.M. Paris time. He said he suddenly realized that all he wanted to do was to go home, finish his last year of college, and get a job. In other words, grow up. He had even taken the responsibility of making a decision that would probably cause some embarrassment since the church was sponsoring his second term in YWAM. He said that admitting he made a mistake in going to France didn't upset him.

I chuckled inwardly as I realized that the Tom coming home was a different person from the little boy running from reality that we left at the airport. Our prayer for Tom when he left had been that God would bring him to maturity. I just didn't expect God to act so quickly! I saw how the fear Tom was manifesting was a classic separation anxiety such as a little child has when separated from its mother. God had to take Tom that far away for me to realize that he was still bonded to me. I know that when I cut the umbilical cord, Tom became a man—a man who could take the responsibility to make a decision and not be afraid to admit he was wrong. He was twenty-one and I guess God decided it was time he grew up.

We need to practice releasing our children to the Lord as they grow up. The first day of school, the first overnight trip away from us, illness, all are opportunities to release our child to the Lord's care. They are preparations for that final release when the child leaves home for marriage or a career.

We can envision the bond as an umbilical cord that binds them to us, a tie that will keep the child from growing into the person God wants him to be. Often, I have a mother who has come for counseling actually picture a cord going from herself to the child. Then I ask her to picture herself cutting that cord and releasing the child to God. The Bible tells us that what we release on this earth is released in heaven (Matthew 16:19; 18:18).

Realize that the habit pattern of protection will also need to be broken and this may take some time. Pray for opportunities to allow your child to venture forth on his own and don't be so quick to always be there for him. Let him ride his bike to the store alone, or make his after-school visit to the orthodontist on his own, provided, of course, it is within a reasonable and safe distance. Encourage him to go on that overnight camping trip or take the job of treasurer of his journalism club, anything that will help him realize his self-sufficiency and potential.

Double-Mindedness

The first chapter of the book of James talks about the type of man whose prayer God honors. He must "ask in faith without any doubting" (verse 6) or he is what James calls "a *double-minded man,* unstable in all his ways" (verse 8; italics mine). Double-minded means literally having two minds. The youngest child has a propensity to this type of instability because of several different factors. We will examine these different factors and see how they contribute to the "double-mindedness" of the youngest.

Misinformation

The main contributing factor to this problem of double-mindedness in youngest children may be connected to the way they receive information from others. Wilson and Edington, two clinical psychologists, have found that the youngest child receives more *mis*information than any other child in the family because most of the things he learns come from other siblings. The older children feel free to check out their perceptions with adults but the youngest "is apt to check with siblings whose pronouncements about the nature of things are often precise, comprehensive, authoritative—and *absolutely incorrect*"[7] (italics mine).

In addition to the misinformation he receives, the youngest child is usually the one "who is ridiculed and put down for not seeing things precisely as others do."[8] After all, it is the youngest who is the last to find out about Santa Claus, the Easter Bunny, and the other mythical figures of childhood. Often the older children lord it over the youngest with winks, giggles, and smug glances.

I can remember the moment when I realized the Easter Bunny was a fictitious animal. I was on my way to bed when I spied a large steaming pot on the stove. I went over and peeked in wondering what Mom was cooking that late at night. The minute I saw the dozens of eggs bubbling away I knew the true identity of the Easter Bunny. Mom asked me not to tell my little sister and I can still remember the knowing glances I kept sending my mother the next morning as Jeannie oohed and aahed over her Easter basket.

Denial

Unfortunately, the youngest often grows up feeling that everyone else knows things he does not. This is not solely the fault of big brothers and sisters: Parents contribute as well. For some reason, most parents feel the "baby" needs to be protected from the problems in the home and so, with the best intentions in the world, they allow him to remain unenlightened. But youngest children are usually "feeling" types who sense emotions in the atmosphere. So even if parents don't tell him that Dad just lost his job, or that they suspect big brother has a drug problem, or that Grandma has just been diagnosed as having cancer, he still senses the anger, hurt, and fear. He begins to doubt his own perceptions and falls into confusion. The result of this protection is that he becomes adept at practicing denial. He develops a method of putting unpleasant things out of his mind and ignoring their existence. This may become a lifelong pattern and any tendency in later life to use drugs and alcohol could stem from this need to reinforce denial. This probably accounts for the fact that more last-borns are likely to be alcoholics than their older siblings.

Friends of ours had a father dying of cancer. He was a youngest child and, for most of his life, an alcoholic. Because of his illness, he could not drink but practiced denial by being the cute little baby clown. He made jokes with the doctors and nurses and it was impossible to hold a serious conversation with him. His three daughters were completely frustrated because he was not a Christian, but every time they tried to talk to him, he would turn it all into a joke.

One night as we were praying for his salvation with his three daughters, who are members of our church, I realized that Mary, the youngest child, was also not facing reality. She had the same fear as her father and they were actually reinforcing one another. She didn't want to face the fact that he was dying, especially since she had lost her mother three years earlier to cancer. I mentioned to her that she was not facing reality in this situation and she began to cry. The other women gathered around Mary and our prayers for her freedom from fear were answered.

The next afternoon I received an excited phone call from Mary. She had just returned from a visit with her father. For the first time she was able to break through his protective wall of joking and talk seriously with him about the Lord. He must have sensed that the fear of facing reality was gone from Mary and that allowed him to be honest about his own fears.

Parents need to be aware that the tendency to protect their youngest from unpleasantness will produce an unstable adult who will not be able to deal with the normal crises of everyday life. This instability just adds to the double-mindedness—wanting to grow up and experience life, but also wanting to deny anything unpleasant.

Self-Doubt

The experience of being on the bottom rung of the birth-order ladder means the youngest never has the experience of seeing a younger sibling going through the same process of learning and understanding new ideas. Because of this, "last-borns as a group tend to suffer serious doubts about their ability to solve problems rationally."[9] Wilson and Edington say that these last-borns are often subject to excruciating episodes of disorientation and self-doubt.

It is easy to see how the last-born's propensity to double-mindedness may develop. The problem is further heightened because the nature of the last child is to withdraw and he keeps his doubts to himself. This gives Satan an ideal access to the mind of the child. If he begins to believe he is unbalanced, Satan's work is then to make the lie a reality. One way out of this is to get the child to begin to talk about the confusion in his mind. The exhortation in James to "confess your sins to one another . . . so that you may be healed" (James 5:16, NIV) is especially relevant for this youngest child. Just knowing other people have often felt the same way is a relief.

Parents should take the time to encourage their youngest children to share their feelings without fear of a putdown remark such as "Oh, you're just being a baby" or "Grow up." These are the types of comments they are used to hearing from older brothers and sisters and part of the reason the youngest child learns to keep his feelings to himself.

As a parent, you may be able to sense when your child needs to talk and perhaps you can pave the way by a question such as "Did you ever wonder if other people thought the same things you do?" or "Did you ever think you were going crazy?" Then you could reassure him that everyone, including yourself, has struggled through times of self-doubt. Teach him to talk out what he is thinking and feeling, and explain that bringing these thoughts into the light takes away the uncertainty that gives Satan his power over us (1 John 1:7). Make sure he understands that these thoughts only have power over us when we keep them to ourselves; once we share them with another person, they lose their power.

Schizophrenia

An extreme form of double-mindedness, or two minds, is schizophrenia. The youngest child makes up a large proportion of the hospital population of schizophrenics[10] and a study of patients suffering from schizophrenia found that "the more older siblings a subject had, as long as she had at least one, the more neurotic, the less self-sufficient, and the less dominant she was likely to be."[11] Each child going down the ladder of birth-order usually becomes less responsible and independent because there are so many older people to take care of his or her needs. This lack of responsibility and self-sufficiency could lead to those feelings of self-doubt that contribute to double-mindedness and, in extreme cases, to schizophrenia.

Researchers in trying to explain the frequency of youngest children, and especially female youngest, in the hospital population of schizophrenics felt that *resentment* of the parents toward the new baby, who may be considered an added burden, partly explained this tendency. The fact that there are more female schizophrenics than male was attributed to the strong parental preference for boys, and hence, more resentment if the "added burden" was a girl.

Researchers also think schizophrenia results from an incomplete separation from the mother: The individual fails to see himself as a separate and distinct entity. As he grows older and begins to leave home, the anxiety of separation from the mother begins to mount. What prevents some mothers from releasing their youngest (or any child) into the freedom of growing into a separate and independent person?

If a mother does feel resentment toward a child, her reaction may be to overprotect the child in an effort to deny her guilt. But the child is the one who suffers. Over-mothering results in a feeble, crippled child who will never grow into adulthood. Subconsciously, this is what the mother wants. She enjoys her children's dependence on her and does not want it to end. The overprotective mother is a selfish mother; she will deny her children the right to grow away from her as she hides her guilt behind the façade of supermom. Youngest children, especially, need to be aware of the tendency to overprotect their children as they were overprotected.

One woman asked me to pray with her because of an inability to release her third child of five. This was the one she had overprotected and couldn't seem to let go of. As we talked, she confessed that the child had been molested when very young by the father. Although she knew of the incident, she had not confronted the father and the guilt she felt because of this situation caused her to want to make up to her child by overprotecting her. Of course we can never make up to our children for our failures, but Jesus can forgive us and heal the wounds.

Justification

The youngest child is often the scapegoat for many of the day-to-day problems in the household and receives more than his share of the blame. Because he is the baby, older siblings feel he is a safe target. Just recently, I was looking for something in the house when my oldest happened to be home. His comment, "Oh, Kelly probably took it," reminded me of the numerous times she had been accused by the others. I guess they figured because she was my baby, I would excuse her, and they were probably right.

Because of being accused so often and the countless put-downs they receive, youngest children become adept at justifying their behavior. They are great manipulators and blame-shifters.

One of the ways that parents can help their youngest, or any of their children, take responsibility is to avoid overprotecting them in relational conflicts. I can remember coming home and complaining about a teacher, friend, or fellow employee. My mother's standard comment was: "I think they are just jealous of you." Then she would go on to reassure me that they were wrong and I was right. As a result, I never learned to take responsibility for my own actions and became great at justification. Several years after I was born again, in the midst of a conflict, I accepted the blame. That was a turning point in my life. Much of my energy had been spent in defending myself and proving that I was right. I found out that my world didn't fall in because I was wrong. In fact, I felt great. There is something liberating in admitting we are wrong. In prayer I went on to tell the Lord I was going to start taking full responsibility for my actions. From that moment I felt I entered the adult world.

Remembering how hard it was for me to learn this, I have tried to help all my children take responsibility especially in the area of relationships. When Kelly would come home from school upset because of some conflict with her teacher or another student, we would sit down and talk it out. Parents have to resist the impulse to say, "Well, what did you do wrong?" This only makes the child defensive. Instead I would ask Kelly to tell me exactly what had happened. As she related the story, I would insert questions like, "How do you think ___ felt when you said that?" or "What do you think your teacher was feeling from your response?" Since youngest children are very empathetic, if we can get them to relate to another's feelings, we can get their thinking off themselves to the other person. Often our discussions would end with Kelly feeling sympathetic toward the one who had offended her and together we would pray for that person.

The youngest or overprotected child has a hard time admitting he is wrong because he already feels so inadequate and is afraid this will make him feel totally inept. If you can gently lead this child to an understanding and admission of his wrongdoing, he will see that this admission brings a good feeling and increases self-esteem. In this way, you will be building good habit patterns of response in the child.

It is easy to understand how the youngest can fall into the pattern of double-mindedness or, in extreme cases, schizophrenia. The misinformation he receives growing up leads him to doubt himself and his powers of rational thinking. His tremendous self-doubt and the family's desire to protect him from anything painful leads him to practice denial which further compounds the problem, since he cannot be truthful and honest about the mental confusion he feels. As he struggles to be free and independent from his mother, he finds himself bound to her and unable to escape. He wants to be free but he fears it; he wants to grow up but he doesn't want to feel the pain of change; he wants to be independent but he likes being protected; he would like to make his own decisions but he doubts his very sanity. He is "driven and tossed by the wind," justifying his every action.

Help for this problem can come only when the whole family sees its part in protecting the baby and allows him to enter fully into the life of the family with his own areas of responsibility and with full knowledge, like the other children, of all the family's tensions.

I believe the majority of Christian parents today love their children deeply and want to give them every advantage so that they will live the abundant life Jesus spoke about. We are shocked by stories of physical and verbal abuse of children and perhaps smugly contemplate our own advantaged offspring. But the truth is that children can be just as damaged by overprotection as they can by physical abuse or neglect. Without sunlight, a plant would wither and die and, in the same way, a baby who cannot connect to a mother will die. But excessive sunlight can kill a plant, too.

We need to find the balance between too little and too much guidance. If we are secure in ourselves, we will allow our children the right to make mistakes because our self-esteem will not be dependent on their performance. We should practice releasing our children from the moment of birth. They are not ours, but God's. Realizing that we are His shepherds but the sheep belong to Him will help us surrender the full weight of responsibility that leads to overprotection.

In the next chapter we are going to consider how the double-mindedness of the youngest child is evident in his emotional life and the way in which God transforms it into a spiritual gift.

Parenting Pointers

1. Do not allow your youngest to sleep in your bed night after night. Parents need to guard their privacy.

2. Mothers must stifle the instinct to always protect their "baby." Although you should guard against domination by the older children, beware of asking others to give in because he/she is the youngest.

3. Train your youngest to fight fear by the use of Scripture. Realize that the tendency to sickness has a root of fear and make sure you are not contributing to the fear.

4. Realize that Mother will eventually have to cut the spiritual umbilical cord that binds her youngest child to herself.

5. Do not always protect your youngest from the tensions within the family. Try to make him feel a part of family situations even if they are unpleasant.

6. Encourage your youngest to talk about his feelings without fear of being ridiculed. Do not let him deny any feelings or problems he may be having.

7. Recognize any resentment you may have had toward this terminal child. Ask forgiveness for your resentment and then accept the child.

8. Help your child talk through relational conflicts. Without accusing him lead him into empathy with the others involved and do not allow him to justify his behavior.

Fourteen

The Emotional Child

Early in childhood, Kelly earned the nickname of Sarah Bernhardt. She had a gift for always dramatizing mundane events into life-or-death situations. My other children would stare after her with lifted eyebrows as she stomped off to her room in anger mumbling about her unfair treatment and then slamming the door for emphasis. Once, to their horror, she even stuck out her tongue at me before she made her dramatic exit. The other children had probably dreamed of doing just that, but never would have dared. On the other hand, she could be gushingly sentimental and teary-eyed over birthdays, Christmas, and even Groundhog's Day, especially if the groundhog did not appear as expected.

The youngest child will usually be the most emotional child in the family for a number of reasons. Youngest children are not taken seriously. Everything they learn has already been learned

175

by their older siblings. Nothing is new for the youngest child; everybody else was already there first. So, if the youngest child is going to stand out in the family, he is going to have to exaggerate the importance of what he does. Because the first day of kindergarten is nothing new to a family with four children, for instance, the youngest will have to embellish this day with some colorful material if he is going to hold the family's interest over the dinner table. This is a skill in which the last child often excels.

Joseph had this same need to be important in the family and it cost him his freedom. Joseph was for many years the youngest of Jacob's eleven sons. His younger brother, Benjamin, was born after Joseph had grown up as the youngest, and Joseph retained the characteristics of the last-born throughout his life. Joseph had a dream from God, but rather than keep it to himself until God brought it to pass, Joseph couldn't resist lording it over his big brothers. After he told them the dream, which depicted his brothers bowing down before him, Scripture says, "they hated him even more" (Genesis 37:8). They already hated him because he was Dad's favorite kid and probably spoiled rotten. He had even been given a multicolored tunic, something their father had not done for any of them. This jealousy was the reason his brothers sold him into slavery.

The Extremist

The situation that Joseph, along with most youngest children, found himself in is the reason for what Wilson and Edington call the "duality" of the youngest child.[1] There is a two-sided element in the nature of the last-born that can swing back and forth many times in the same day. The youngest child can be cheerful and on top of the world in the morning and by lunchtime, down in the pits of depression. She can be full of energy, ready to tackle anything one minute, and totally lethargic, sitting and staring at the TV screen the next. He may feel like God's gift to the world one day and a total failure the next.

Much of this emotional see-sawing comes from the way the last-born is treated growing up. There are those who spoil and overprotect this youngest child and those who dominate and mistreat him. Joseph had on the one hand the indulgence of his father that made him feel like a prince and on the other hand the hatred of his older brothers that made him feel like a pauper. Where was his true identity?

Sometimes the lines are not so clearly drawn. The same people who spoil and overprotect the child one minute may put him down and make fun of him the next. It seems the youngest not only receives more than his fair share of pampering but also of teasing. It is easy to see how these contradictory signals coming from those who are supposed to love and care for him cause confusion and emotional turmoil in the mind of the last-born.

The extremism typical of this birth order is usually more severe in the case of the youngest male. We are more consistently overindulgent with a youngest girl, the little princess of the family. When the youngest is a boy, the line of demarcation between those who tolerate and those who dominate is more clearly drawn. This results in a personality characterized by extremes.

King David was the youngest of Jesse's eight sons and it is easy to see the extremism of his emotions by reading the Psalms. David might be praising the Lord from a mountaintop experience in one psalm and in the pit of despondency begging for mercy in the next. He could dance before the Lord in joyous freedom (2 Samuel 6:14, 20) or he could fast and lie prostrate on the ground before the Lord in repentence as he did for the child born to him and Bathsheba (2 Samuel 12:16). Joseph was equally emotional. At one point, when he was reunited with his brothers, he cried so loudly that the entire household of Pharaoh heard him (Genesis 45:1–2). Also, when Joseph met his father, Israel, again, the Bible tells us that he wept a long time (Genesis 46:29). Who but a youngest child could be so free and spontaneous with his emotions? David and Joseph had a depth and richness of emotion unequaled by other Old Testament heroes.

Wilson and Edington say that one way parents can help the youngest, or any child, rocked by extremism of emotions is through regular routines.[2] Setting definite times for going to bed and getting up in the morning, mealtimes, studying, and exercise. These little routines are especially helpful during emotional crises when the world seems so insecure. I've often thought it interesting that, as soon as Jesus raised Jairus' daughter from the dead, he ordered them to give her something to eat (Luke 8:40–56). I'm sure her mother and father were in a state of shock but the simple act of preparing food was able to bring them back to reality. In the same way, little routines and rituals can be comforting to children as long as they don't become a slave to routine. Routine can give us a sense of security but we must not put our security in the routine.

Parents can also help the emotional child find balance by being more consistent in their discipline. To allow the youngest or any child "to get away with murder" one time because she is so cute, and then punish her the next for the same offense, contributes to this extremism and causes the older children to feel the youngest is being favored. What parent has not heard this retort from their older children: "You let him/her get away with murder. You never let me do those things"? Unfortunately, it is usually true.

It is an established fact that the youngest child who needs the most discipline receives the least. If we could have our last child first, the problem would be solved but it doesn't work that way. "Why make a fuss about the little things?" became my motto with the last baby. "I am going to enjoy her." I did enjoy her but at the expense of teaching her some needed discipline.

Many youngest children grow up feeling life is totally out of their control because the parents and older siblings take so much responsibility away from them. It is interesting that, particularly among women, self-discipline over food is related to the amount of control a person feels over her life. And it is often women who were the youngest in the family who have the hardest time controlling their weight. "Baby fat" is more than just a cute jibe. Often it is an unpleasant reality for many who are the baby: the less control, the more fat. In this context we see anorexia among teenage girls as an extreme fear of being out of control. The first step for the youngest child who fights a weight problem may, again, be to help her establish daily routines.

Relating to Others

The last-born sibling in the birth-order configuration is a "people person" par excellence. Because he is the smallest, weakest, and least knowledgeable in the family, he tends to develop his interpersonal skills—powers of negotiation, accommodation, tolerance, and a capacity to accept less favorable outcomes—to a greater degree than any other child in the family. Because of this knowledge of human relationships that the youngest child acquires, it is not surprising that he is found to be the most popular child among peers. [3]

The first child functions in ideas, middle children can move back and forth in the world of ideas and emotions, the youngest child often functions totally in emotions. The members of our church all took the Meyers-Briggs Personality Test recently. This test measures four functions, one of which is thinking versus feeling. Of all the youngest in our church, only two scored on the thinking side. The others were all motivated by feelings and some, like my youngest sister, Jeannie, scored twenty points for feeling and zero points for thinking. Jeannie's husband, Ken, on reading her score said laughingly, "That's the last time I ask her what she thinks!"

Initially, all children relate on an emotional level. They are more tuned in to how they feel than what they think. That is why it is useless for parents to go through prolonged explanations to a three-year-old about the pros and cons of a situation. At this age their minds have not developed the ability to think conceptually. In fact, most psychologists feel that abstract thinking does not develop till the child is about twelve years old. Before that time, the child is limited in his thinking to concrete, or nonsymbolic, terms.

Even though the last-born's cognitive thinking pattern does develop, this child, or another child in the family who is the emotional child, remains tuned in to his emotions.

I am primarily a thinking person as measured by the personality test and, for the first time, I understood the conflict between myself and my youngest child. I would sit down with her and try to talk rationally about a situation while she was responding emotionally. We were communicating on two different levels and seeing things from different perspectives. I had no trouble relating to my first two children, who are primarily thinking types, but I had difficulty with my two youngest who are feeling types.

One friend of mine, who is the youngest child in the family, came to me with a concern about her oldest son. "He seems to have no mercy or tolerance for others," was her complaint. Her situation was just the opposite of mine. As a youngest child, she was a "feeling" person, and her oldest son was an "idea" person. They were both coming from their basic gift and seeing the other's weakness. She was trying to relate to him from her emotional perspective and he needed someone to relate to him on a logical level.

My mother was also a youngest child and we had many disagreements over this same point. She would decide to do or not do something on the basis of how she felt. "I don't feel like it," was her favorite expression and one that drove me crazy. "We don't do things because we feel like it, but because we are committed to it," was my standard reply. Then the argument began and always ended in a stalemate. Unfortunately (or fortunately) oldest and youngest children usually marry and then the battle begins.

If there is one desire the youngest child will almost always have it is the need for their strong emotions to be understood. When

I realized this I changed my approach to Kelly and to those from this birth-order position who come to me for counseling. If, for instance, Kelly comes home upset because of some situation at school or in her job, I don't lecture her on her responsibility or throw some worn cliché at her. Instead I try to relate to what she is feeling and respond with something like: "You must have been really hurt by what she said" or "I would have been embarrassed if that happened to me" or "Didn't you feel angry inside?" Once youngest children realize that you understand how they are feeling, they are more open to discussing the right response. In fact, Kelly often comes up with a good solution.

This type of communication works equally well with all our children, especially when they are young. As I mentioned before, young children respond initially on an emotional or feeling level so we need to let them know we understand what they are feeling before we can help them overcome these emotions. Often parents are too quick to judge the behavior without actually understanding the strong emotions that are behind the behavior. If the oldest child in the family is displaying jealousy toward the new baby, it is useless to tell him, "You shouldn't feel that way toward your baby sister." If on the other hand the mother were to say, "I bet you wish you were a little baby again with everyone fussing over you" or "You probably feel jealous because everyone is bringing the new baby gifts," this would tell your child you understand the turmoil he is feeling and you still love and accept him. In this way you help him identify his feelings and thereby diminish their intensity.

Showing our children that we understand what they are feeling is like defusing a bomb. If we try to give them advice or criticism before we deal with their emotions, we'd better be prepared for the explosion. Even when a child makes negative statements about himself, it is pointless to try to argue with him. For instance, if your child says, "I can never do anything right," you will not convince him by reasoning that he can. He is in the midst of a strong feeling and is not open to logic. If you were to respond with, "I know how you feel, I have days when I feel like that too" or "Nothing seems to be going right today," you are identifying with him in his emotion and this in itself relieves some of the pressure. You will be surprised at the change in attitude when your child realizes you do understand what he is feeling.

Anger

The youngest child, if a boy, has an especially difficult time. This sensitivity to the spirit and feelings of others is acceptable in girls in our society but not in boys. A youngest boy would be ridiculed and put down by older siblings if he revealed his emotional nature. Because of this he has to bottle up his true feelings and let them come out another way. One of those ways is anger. The youngest child, whether boy or girl, may either vent his anger in frequent, volatile tirades or turn it inward and handle it with passive-aggressive behavior.

Passive-aggressive behavior is a way of getting back at someone in an indirect way. Often, the child is not even aware that he is using this type of anger to get back at his parents. Some examples are procrastination, forgetfulness, and stubbornness. One of the earliest ways that Kelly showed this type of anger was by wetting the bed at night. We tried everything to break this habit in her— no drinks before bedtime, waking her up before we went to bed— but to no avail. She had this problem till she was about six.

She was basically a happy child and I didn't realize that I was reinforcing this passive-aggressive behavior by not allowing her to express her anger, which could be explosive. My other three children fought with each other as a way of expressing their anger. Kelly was too young to be considered one of the group and so she didn't have this release.

In high school she was our most obedient child except for one rather perplexing problem. She was habitually late coming in on the weekends. She didn't understand why she did this and even asked me to pray about it. We came to see this was her passive-aggressive way of showing anger. Some teenagers may do poorly in school, use alcohol or drugs, drive recklessly, commit vandalism, or even suicide as a way of expressing their anger.

If we are going to help our children deal with their anger, we first have to acknowledge and learn to deal constructively with our own. Since my father was easily angered I grew up afraid of his outbursts and, therefore, afraid to recognize anger in myself. Instead, I turned it inward and suffered physically. Oldest and youngest children are probably most prone to anger—the oldest because he bears the brunt of the discipline in the family and the youngest because of his deep-rooted sense of fear and insecurity. Christian parents especially are often guilty of causing their children to deny or suppress their anger because "it isn't the Christian thing to do." This type of attitude is disastrous to the child.

The first step is to help your children identify the emotion as anger, and the second is to help them understand why they are angry. I found exercise helpful in dealing with anger—not as a way to deny it, but rather to get rid of the overwhelming emotion so I could get a handle on the reason for the anger. My son Tom would go down into the basement and play his drums quite vigorously to work out his feelings when he was angry. After your children understand *why* they are angry, it is easier to yield the anger to God and ask His help in dealing with it.

Whether your child explodes or denies his anger, you have the opportunity to help him learn self-control. First, your attitude toward anger should demonstrate to your child that you accept it as a normal human emotion but that God wants us to harness it. We are not to be angerless people but people who have the righteous anger of God toward evil. Encourage your youngest that his strong feelings and emotions can be used by God; they just have to be directed in the proper chanels.

Spiritual Gifts

Because youngest children remain motivated primarily by their emotions, they usually have gifts of mercy or serving. Both of these gifts are directly related to helping people. Older children in the birth-order constellation possess gifts of teaching, exhortation, prophecy, and organization. They are more concerned with ideas, rules, laws, justice, and efficient functioning. But later-born children care about people and will even bend the rules rather than risk hurting a relationship. You can imagine the conflict within the Body of Christ between those who show mercy and those who are prophets—one is interested in people and one in principles.

Those who have the gift of serving are those who are able to see the practical needs of people, have a strong desire to be with others, enjoy the constant change of short-range goals or projects, and feel unqualified for spiritual leadership. Youngest children simply because of their coming last have had ample opportunity to learn servanthood. Usually the youngest child has been everybody's "go-for" and this is his way to earn the respect and love of others.

Kelly's desire to serve became apparent when she was quite young. At church meetings Kelly loved to pass out song sheets, name cards, and anything else that needed to be distributed. She especially enjoyed dinner parties at our home and I would let her stay up later than her normal bedtime to help me serve the guests. Sometimes she was more of a hindrance than a help but I recognized her desire to serve and see now this probably was her spiritual gift. If you believe one of your children has the gift of serving, you need to let him express this gift even if it means extra work for you. These children are usually excited at the prospect of company coming and are good at remembering little things about people and their likes and dislikes. They may remember Aunt Mary loved the broccoli casserole you made last time she came to dinner, or know exactly the right gift to buy for cousin Sara's birthday.

The gift of serving is closely allied with the gift of mercy and sometimes difficult to tell apart. Both desire to show love to the other person, but serving demonstrates that love by meeting practical needs while mercy desires to meet emotional needs. You can see why the youngest child is especially motivated in these areas.

As Kelly grew older and especially when she entered high school, I began to detect that her gift might fit more into the category of mercy. Problem people were drawn to Kelly as if they could sense her acceptance and concern. Other students would tell her things about themselves that they would not share with anyone else. She is a good listener and deeply touched by the problems of others. She has decided to go into counseling since she feels this is the way she can best help those with personal problems.

It is interesting that those with the gift of mercy are often attracted to those with the gift of prophecy. I mentioned in a previous chapter that the second child is often a prophet. In a session I had with those who are the youngest in their families, all of them said that they were either married to a second-born or that their best friends were from the ranks of the second-born. Every boy Kelly has ever been attracted to has turned out to be a second-born; it's almost as if we sense what we need to be kept in balance.

Parents need to be sensitive to their child's spiritual bent and encourage him or her in that direction. Otherwise the child may grow up frustrated and living out an unfulfilling role. When a young woman named Kathy came to our church a number of years ago, I was impressed with the tremendous ministry of serving that she and her husband, Phil, a pediatrician, had to the students of a local medical school. One thing puzzled me about Kathy, though, and that was her tendency to tears at the slightest provocation. My husband and I had the opportunity to spend some good fellowship time with them and during our conversations we discovered the root of her problem.

Kathy was an achieving first-born girl. Her mother had been a later-born daughter and had a wonderful gift of mercy. "All sorts of people found their way to my mom's kitchen," Kathy told us, "and she fed and loved them all." Because the first-born is especially motivated to imitate the mother, Kathy tried to follow her mother's example of serving and mercy. Kathy's gift, however, was prophecy and she had to squelch her real desires continually to play the role she thought should be hers. This frustration led to those frequent tears. The prophet enjoys long-range goals and sees suffering as a means to an end. The one who shows mercy wants to relieve suffering immediately by administering physical or emotional comfort. It is easy to see why Kathy was so frustrated. Once she was free to be herself, the tears ceased to flow so easily.

The opposite situation led Helen to cry easily in frustration. She was the fourth and youngest raised in a cold, critical family. She is a sensitive and tender person but was not allowed to show her concern at home for fear of teasing and ridicule. She, too, learned to squelch her natural tendencies. Once we realized her true gift, we encouraged her to begin to react from deep within her spirit rather than the way she felt others wanted her to be.

The youngest child can be a delightful child if allowed to express himself emotionally. Just because he is last in no way means he is least. God has given him a depth and sensitivity that no other child in the family can attain. We have to be careful to guard his tender and compassionate nature and yet not overprotect him. On the other hand, if we view emotional people as weak and indecisive, we will not let this child develop in the way that God has planned for him. First-born parents especially will have a hard time understanding their youngest. This may be why

God had to remove both Joseph and David from their families for many years before He could give them leadership.

In the next chapter we are going to discuss the goals and achievements of youngest children and how parents can encourage them to find God's plan for their lives.

Parenting Pointers

1. Be consistent in your discipline. Do not allow older siblings to dominate or pamper the youngest.

2. Help your youngest establish regular routines and stick to them.

3. Try to understand what your child is feeling emotionally and convey that to him before you attempt to give advice or correction.

4. Give your youngest opportunities to serve others but do not allow him to be treated as everybody's "go-for."

5. If your youngest has a gift of mercy, realize that he/she will be especially sensitive to his own feelings and those of others. Do not convey the idea that sensitive people are weak or emotional. Rather encourage him with stories of David and Joseph.

6. Help your child to deal constructively with his anger. That means learning to recognize it, understanding why, and then yielding it to God.

Fifteen

The Baby Grows Up

The youngest child enters a world where everyone has gone before. Every accomplishment, suggestion, and activity of the youngest child has been experienced by the parents, who, by this time, are getting pretty tired of trying to look excited about a Christmas ornament made out of a used spool of thread. When the last child moves onto the scene, parents have become experts at ignoring his questions and observations while repeating phrases like, "Hmm," "Not now," "Maybe," and "We'll see." The youngest isn't fooled. He knows that no one listens to him but he keeps talking in the hope that someday. . . . And then he realizes that if he is going to get his fair share of attention, it is going to have to be in ways other than striving for achievement. Let firstborn take the lion's share of the acclamation for achievement; baby will settle for the love and attention of the parents and the older siblings.

It's up to parents to help their youngest child develop motivation to achieve as he grows up. And since he desires attention, the best way to stimulate him is through constructive praise.

Praise

All children are stimulated by praise but the youngest is especially motivated. Constructive praise can cause a youngest child to redouble his efforts. I saw this in action once when a friend of ours, who grew up the youngest child of five, was putting in a new lawn. He took a week's vacation time to do it and, at our Sunday night house church meeting, I asked him if he had completed the back-breaking job. He replied that he had finished that day and added cheerfully that it hadn't been nearly as bad as he had feared. He then went on to tell me how his wife and each one of his four children had come out periodically to inspect the job or to bring him a glass of lemonade. Every time they came out they praised his work. "That praise literally kept me going," he said with a big smile on his face. "Every time I felt like quitting, I remembered what they said and that helped me finish."

Praise can literally keep a youngest child going—*if* we know how to give it. Believe it or not, praise can be destructive and result in bad behavior. In order for praise to build up a child's confidence it should be given for accomplishments and not for character or personality traits.

For instance, to tell a child, "You are such a good little girl," is unrealistic and destructive. The child will immediately remember all the times she wasn't such a good little girl like the time she stole her little sister's candy or hated her dad for spanking her. Then, to prove she isn't really such a good little girl and to get rid of the guilt, she may misbehave and the parent is left confused.

Instead, praise should be specific. If, for instance, Jimmy picks up all the toys in the family room and puts them in the toy box, it would be appropriate to say, "You sure got those toys picked up in a hurry," or "The family room looks nice and neat now that you picked up all your toys." Jimmy can accept this praise because it is for a specific task. It would be inappropriate to say, "You always do such a good job" because Jimmy knows he doesn't.

Best-selling author Cecil Osborne relates the tale of a woman in her mid-thirties, dying of cancer. She felt that there was a definite relationship between her illness and her mother's attitude. She said her mother always insisted her children were perfect. Responding to that unrealistic praise, she said, "We all tried to live up to that. We knew that we weren't perfect, of course, and I think this created a terrible conflict between the knowledge that we were imperfect kids like everyone else and the goal of perfection that Mother set for us. I feel that this conflict I have lived with so long is somehow related to my cancer."[1]

My mother gave us the same type of unrealistic praise. When I came home with my class picture, she would study it and then say, "You are the prettiest little girl in the class." I can remember reacting angrily inside when she said that but not understanding why. My mother was telling me something nice and I didn't like her for it. Since she always gave us praise in general terms, "You are the smartest; you did the best job; you sang the best in the play," I spent a lot of time feeling confused about my reactions and finally convinced myself that I must be a very evil child to react so negatively to kind words. Her praise had exactly the opposite effect from what she intended. I know my mother had only my best interest at heart when she made these statements and in her eyes I probably was the smartest, the prettiest, etc., but it always left me wondering. Why did she have to pretend? The conclusion I finally came to was that she couldn't accept me the way I was and was trying to make me something I wasn't. Praise is a powerful force for motivating our children but like dynamite, it must be handled properly or it could blow up in our faces.

Achievement

No matter how much you praise and encourage your youngest child, though, don't expect him to become achievement-oriented in the same way as the older children. Since our own definition of achievement will vary according to our birth order, we have to understand what is most important to our children and not try to make them conform to our ideas of success. God has put a special gift within each of our children and it is our task to steer them in God's direction, not our ideas of His direction.

When Kelly was in high school, the grades on her report card could vary from A to D. There didn't seem to be any pattern either. She would get a good grade in chemistry one semester and a bad grade the next. This had me puzzled until I realized that her grade was dependent, not so much on the course of study, but on the teacher. If she liked the teacher, and felt the teacher also liked her, she would be motivated to achieve. Any praise the teacher gave her would cause her to redouble her efforts in class even if she didn't care for the subject. On the other hand, if she felt the teacher didn't like her for some reason, she wouldn't even try. It is important for parents to understand this: Youngest children, while seeking admiration and affection, will practically knock themselves out to prove themselves to someone who gives them attention.

One teacher was responsible for a big change in Kelly in high school. During her junior year, she began writing for the high school paper. She and the journalism teacher hit it off immediately. This teacher conveyed to Kelly that she thought she had potential and Kelly began to work to prove her friend was right. Each semester her grades went up till she made the honor roll. During her senior year, she not only wrote in-depth articles for the paper, but also became their chief photographer. Her teacher told me she was a "one-man newspaper" and often her hard work was the thing that got the newspaper out on time.

When it came time for my oldest to go to college, his choice was motivated by the school's academic reputation. Kelly's motivation for choosing a college was much different. She was more interested in the environment and the friendliness of the students. If parents don't understand their youngest child, they may look on these qualifications as frivolous. But a school setting is important to the youngest child and must mirror the warmth and friendliness of home. Youngest children will try to make their dorm rooms very comfortable and reminiscent of home with a lot of what parents would call "junk," but if the atmosphere isn't right, the youngest child will feel disoriented.

We went down to Kelly's future college for a two-day orientation and registration. As we were riding home, Kelly told me she had signed up for ten clubs—three Christian organizations, one helping the handicapped, photography, etc. Her dad and I laughed about this and decided maybe we wouldn't have her sign up for classes her second semester as they would interfere with her social life. Although we joked about it, this illustrates an important facet of the youngest child's makeup and one that cannot be overlooked.

Unfortunately, in our achievement-oriented country, success in relationships is not considered success at all. This is why the youngest child often feels like a failure intellectually. In Kelly's case it was pretty hard for her to understand that her gifts were important—especially since she had an older brother in medical school and an older sister in law school. But parents need to convey to their children who are talented in working with people that this is just as much an achievement as straight A's on a report card, and then direct them into fields of study that can utilize their strengths. A child psychologist friend of mine once told me that wise children often don't do well in school because they see no purpose for many of the classes. Later-born children can fall into this category.

While visiting Kelly's college, we were continually reminded that employers are looking for graduates who can write fluently and who can speak before groups. With all our specialized academic training, we have failed to produce people who can communicate. Youngest children are experts in communication and in this sense they will have an advantage in today's job market. Writers, musicians, artists, and language majors all come mainly from the ranks of later-born children.

An interesting study of our American presidents found that the majority have been either the oldest child in the family or the oldest male child.[2] Only three presidents were youngest children: William Henry Harrison, Andrew Johnson, and James Garfield. Interestingly, of these three, two died within five months of their inauguration and the third was impeached. Youngest children normally do not like the full load of responsibility on their shoulders. Actually, it may be that youngest children are too smart to desire high office. Let big brother kill himself in his attempt to achieve power; little brother wants time to smell the roses. Life is more than work, striving for power, and drudgery for the youngest child. The author of the article about the presidents says that the oldest is most likely to be president, the middle child is more suited to the office of prime minister, and the youngest son, unsuited for practical affairs, should be a philosopher king. He concludes that the youngest is not likely ever to be president and "so much the sadder for the nation."

One of the greatest problems for the youngest child is his ambivalence about becoming an adult. On the one hand, he wants to grow up to attain his share of the privileges reserved for the big people but he also likes the idea of being the baby and the attention he receives by being weak and helpless. Often the latter wins out. Mothers especially are only too eager to do for baby what we expected our other children to do for themselves. Since we are a big part of the problem we are also the major part of the solution.

I often typed out Kelly's term papers the night before so that she could get her proper sleep. I didn't have the time to do this for the older chilren and, when I realized I was doing Kelly a disservice by helping her, I let her do her own papers even if she did them at the last minute. When mothers are too quick to help our youngest out of a situation, we are really saying, "You are too weak and helpless to do this on your own so I will do it for you." Rather than helping the child, it just convinces her that she really doesn't have what it takes to make it in the real world.

The butterfly has to struggle out of the cocoon, the chicken needs to peck his way out of the shell, and baby, to be successful in life, has to learn to get out of his own situations. Most of us want to protect our children from failure but failure is an important step in the growing-up process. Failure isn't harmful to a child. It is the *fear* of failure that paralyzes, and that is what mothers convey to our children when we are too quick to step in and do for them. We are teaching them that they must avoid failure at all costs.

The Caboose Baby

The caboose baby or "change-of-life baby" is a child born many years after the next-oldest brother or sister. Often the child is an "accident" and, although the parents may later find this child is the joy of their lives, the first reaction to the pregnancy is usually anger and resentment. For these reasons, this child may spend the rest of his life trying "to avoid further displeasing or inconveniencing anyone."[3] It's as if he is trying to make up to his parents and the world for his birth. As mentioned in the previous chapter, parents need to pray and ask forgiveness for this attitude and release the child from a spirit of rejection.

One friend of Kelly's, who was born when her parents were in their late forties, reacted to this rejection by becoming disobedient and rebellious. Her parents responded in turn by being overly permissive to cover the guilt they felt because of their resentment over her birth. The result was disaster. The girl began using drugs while still in grammar school and later became pregnant and had to quit high school. We can never cover over our original resentment by permissiveness, love, or material gifts. It is like a festering splinter and has to be removed. Otherwise, the child senses our guilt and plays on it, manipulating us to make up to her. The only way out of such a situation is to go back to the original feelings, ask forgiveness, and accept our child. Then, God can truly restore the bad years (Joel 2:25).

This type of last-born child has grown up in a house where even the older brothers and sisters acted like parents. It is difficult enough to grow up with all older brothers and sisters but when they are almost adults, it brings a great deal of confusion because of the mixed messages coming from all the different people in the house. In this type of situation, parents would need to see that the child wasn't excessively dominated or pampered by the older siblings. Also, as we shall see next with the only child, this child needs to spend time with friends his own age or younger to sharpen his skills in competition and leadership.

The two adjectives that I have found in my research that most frequently are applied to youngest children are *delightful* and *charming*. If first-borns are the trailblazers on the road of life, last-borns are the ones who plant the flowers along the way. They may not accomplish the great feats of their older brothers or sisters but they surely make life a lot more enjoyable for the rest of us. The older I get, the more I realize, along with the author of Ecclesiastes, the vanity of life. Often, the things we call achievement are especially vain. Kelly has helped her striving second-born mother realize that life is too short to spend all of it reaching for those things the world has decided are important. She has helped me to understand the importance of relationships and of just enjoying the world God has created for us. Youngest children can bring joy and creativity to the natural family and the family of God, if their older siblings will realize they *can* learn from the baby.

Parenting Pointers

1. Be specific in your praise of your child's accomplishments. For example, say, "Sharing your candy with your friend was a kind thing to do," not, "You are a kind girl."

2. Realize the importance of the teacher-student relationship in the life of your youngest child. If there is an unresolvable conflict, request a transfer.

3. Recognize that relationships may be more important to your youngest child than achievement and help him to see the value in that.

4. Try to stimulate your youngest child's creativity in writing, art, or music.

5. Don't allow your youngest to manipulate you into doing his homework. He needs to find out his own capabilities.

Sixteen

That Special
Only Child

At the turn of the century, G. Stanley Hall, the dean of American psychologists, said: "Being an only child is a disease in itself." Since that time, parents have come to feel that they have to have a second child if only to save their first. Only children were common in the Depression years but after World War II came the baby boom and a new emphasis on family life.

Today, the average number of children per family has dipped below two for the first time in decades (1.85 in 1985) and only children are far more common. In 1985 there were thirteen million only children in this country—about fifty percent more than twenty years ago.[1] Because of the growing number of onlies, psychologists have recently completed numerous studies on the only child and discovered that most of the negative attitudes toward the one-child family are unjustified.

Years ago, if a couple had an only child it was usually because they were unable to have another due to medical complications. But today, the reasons for having one child are more of choice. Many only children have parents who both work full-time and are concerned about having enough money for more than one child. Also, more couples are in their thirties today when they begin their families and it may be too late to start considering a second child. Another reason may be that more than thirty-five percent of only children come from divorced families and the couples weren't together long enough to have more than one child.[2]

Because of this decline in the birth rate, we may soon be a society of onlies, first-borns, and second-borns. Many psychologists feel that our culture will suffer if it loses the leavening influence of the middle child. Society will become more driving and perfectionistic due to the influence of the only and first children. If we are heading toward a society with many only children then we had better understand the difficulties as well as the advantages in the one-child family.

The only child is not only his parents' first child but also the youngest. We would, therefore, expect him to have many of the same characteristics of these two birth orders. Like first-borns, onlies are over-represented in the upper IQ group and among the students in colleges and universities with high entrance requirements and also in professional schools, so the same danger of too much pressure for achievement is common with onlies. And since the only is also his parents' youngest, he is often overprotected. Because the only child grows up without siblings, there are some major differences in his personality, however, and it is these differences that we are going to consider.

The Long-Awaited Special Child

Like all first-born children, the only child is greeted by two parents who have been anxiously awaiting his birth. If the child is born to older parents, after a previous miscarriage or a long wait, the anxiety may be acute. Then all their love, care, attention, and discipline is focused on this first child: Nothing is too difficult for the parents and nothing is too good for this special child.

With other first-borns, the arrival of the second child defocuses some of this attention. The only child, however, remains in the spotlight for the rest of his life. He doesn't have any siblings to help give his parents the perspective they need on the expectations they have for this child. Parents with several children can see their successes as well as their failures but the parents of a single child don't have this perspective. Their only child is the singular example of their success as parents: He will prove or disprove their skills and capabilities. Everything is riding on him and he knows it.

Parents' Two Mistakes

Parents of only children may respond two ways: They may, one, overindulge or, two, dominate. Dr. David Levy says that the fundamental temperament of the child determines the way the parents respond.[3] If the child is rebellious and aggressive, the parents will give in and indulge him. If he is quiet and submissive, his parents will continue to exercise control.

In meeting with a group of only children, Dave was the most extreme example of a child whose parents overindulged. There seemed to be two main reasons for their overindulgence: Dave was adopted, and the adoption took place after the death of his parents' only natural child. Adoptive parents usually feel they have to prove they are worthy to be parents and go overboard in an effort to please their child. And the death of the natural child only increased their anxiety and guilt. Dave fed on their indulgence and, from the age of ten, did exactly what he wanted.

Unfortunately, their permissiveness had devastating results. Since Dave did not have authority figures in his life whom he trusted and respected, he felt totally alone when he faced the problems of adolescence. This was probably the reason he started taking drugs at the age of twelve. He spent the next twenty-four years in bondage to drugs and alcohol until at the age of thirty-six he accepted Christ and was released from his prison of addiction. Dave still has trouble trusting others but has learned to submit to advice and counsel from those people he knows God has put in authority.

Unlike Dave most of the onlies in the group described themselves as quiet children with controlling parents. The most misguided of this type of parent, in an effort to spare his child all possibly harmful situations, will respond the opposite of Dave's parents and attempt to make every decision for the child. Parents of only children are also noted for forever warning them of the hazards that await beyond the threshold of their home. These constant warnings fill the child with anxiety, and reinforce his inability to make any decision for fear of danger or failure. Interestingly, like Dave, in some cases the pressure of excessive dominance also result in the child's rebellion later in life.

We have been friends with a single-child family for a number of years and it has been interesting to observe. The mother is a domineering first child and she has established rules for every area of the son's life, including his play. Although they have a swimming pool, he can only use it in accordance with a strict set of rules. It must be at least a half hour after a meal, she must be present to watch, if he is getting tired he has to come out and rest, and on and on. As you can imagine, this has become something of a neighborhood joke. Of course, "Mom knows best" and is just trying to make life easier for her son but all this guidance just convinces him that he is totally unable to make any meaningful decisions.

I'm sure this mother, like all overprotective mothers, is motivated by love but it is a selfish kind of love that will not allow the child to become independent and responsible. As we saw with the last-born it also ensures that the child will remain dependent on her. Every person has to learn to make his own decisions and also to live with the consequences of those decisions. If we make all the decisions for our child, either he will grow up an indecisive adult who has a fear of failure, or he may decide to rebel against the domination when he reaches adolescence. Because the parents of only children often set such rigid rules, the child may feel that rebellion is the only way he can break that bondage. If the parents were to lighten up on their control, the only wouldn't have to rebel so violently to break free.

Is your child quiet and passive? Does he avoid confrontation? Does he always gives in to other children? Is he indecisive or overly cautious? Does he accept your rules and authority without ever reacting? Is he a loner? If your answer is yes to the majority of these questions, then you may be in danger of stifling your only child through your domination.

The Right Response

Dr. Murray Kappelman, in his book *Raising the Only Child*, says that the key to a successful relationship between the only child and his parents is a clear understanding of the rules and appropriate punishments for misbehavior.[4] Without adequate discipline, a child will not be prepared for the outside world. Teachers, friends, and employers will not be as indulgent as Mom and Dad.

Because the interaction between the parents and child is at a maximum, the balance is crucial. Children need to be encouraged to make their own decisions quite young—what toy to play with, which friend to invite over—and to live with wrong choices. At the same time they need to live within a structure of rules that will give them security but not stifle their individuality.

Discipline also needs to be consistent because the only child does not have siblings to observe in disciplinary situations. Within a large family, children often learn from watching brothers and sisters undergo discipline. The single child has no such advantage. Because of that, if discipline is not consistent, the child will become confused. Kelly, our youngest, has often commented that she learned what *not* to do by watching the other children. Tom's problem with drugs especially convinced her that she never wanted to experiment with them. Because of this, she had an easy time saying no to that temptation in high school.

One thing I have noticed about the young families in our fellowship is that so many of the mothers (and fathers) are intimidated by their children. Most are not convinced that it is loving to discipline their children, and have a hard time saying no. Perhaps the fact that they are Christians is part of the problem; the realization of the tremendous responsibility they have as parents produces fear of making the wrong decisions. The book of Hebrews says that ". . . those whom the Lord loves He disciplines, And He scourges every son whom He receives" (Hebrews 12:6, NAS). Consistent discipline produces a secure child because he understands that the rules don't change on the whim of a parent.

Because parents of an only child have no previous experience in discipline and no later children to put things into perspective, this is going to be a difficult area to bring into balance. Recognizing this at the beginning and studying Christian books on children and discipline will be helpful. The balance between too little and too much is important, but even more important is the agreement between the parents. Nothing is more confusing to a child than parents arguing about his discipline. He learns to play one against the other. This breeds tremendous insecurity in the child and will only cause him later in life to have a hard time finding security in God. Both parents must agree on the rules and also the punishment for breaking the rules. It is common for an only child to withdraw after a period of discipline. There is nothing wrong in this and should be allowed if the withdrawal doesn't extend beyond a reasonable time.

Unrealistic Expectations

Parents who have more than one child get used to the variation of abilities in their children. One child may be a good student, another may be an athlete, and a third may be artistically creative. Parents of the only child, though, may find it difficult to objectively evaluate their child's potential. Recently, the father of an only child was relating his four-year-old daughter's amazing vocabulary. After he walked away, a mother of three remarked to me, "It's a shame he doesn't realize his daughter is just a normal kid. I'm afraid he's going to be very disappointed when she starts school."

Since the parents of only children tend to overestimate their child's abilities, this, of course, places a tremendous pressure on the only child to achieve. Only children, like first-borns, thrive on adult approval. If parents set consistently unrealistic goals for their children, they are predisposing them to failure. Dr. Kappelman reports that "a significant proportion of school phobias, unexplained failures, drop-outs, and outstanding students who suddenly cave in emotionally are only children."[5]

Because of the parental pressure to achieve, onlies, like first-borns, are often perfectionists.

Lucille Forer, in *The Birth Order Factor*, says that "mothers of only sons often attribute 'miracle making' powers to their children. . . ."[6] In addition they frequently praised and encouraged their sons. Because of this many only men have the attitude that "I'm Number One." In fact, in a group of male onlies I met with one evening, all related this attitude. Steve told us his parents convinced him he could be the best at anything he undertook. He said this became the driving force in his life and he still can't tolerate people who don't strive and do their best.

The child perceives his parents to be as wise and all-knowing as God. If the parent tells the child he can be the best, the child assumes this is so—and that being the best is important. What happens, though, if the child is not equipped physically or intellectually to be the best? His parents couldn't be wrong in their expectations, he figures, so there must be something wrong with him: He is a failure.

When the patriarch Jacob was dying, he summoned all his sons so that he could prophesy over each of them. His prophecy over Reuben the first-born is descriptive of all first children and especially applies to the only child:

> Reuben, you are my first-born, my might, and the first fruits of my strength, pre-eminent in pride and pre-eminent in power. *Unstable as water* . . . (Genesis 49:3–4, RSV, italics added).

I believe the phrase "unstable as water" refers to the extremism of first children. Water can change from a liquid to a solid, from hot to cold, just as the first child can be a super-achiever or a total burnout. The only child, like all first-borns, wants to please his parents and win their approval, but if they set consistently unrealistic goals for him, he will drop out altogether.

The other danger in constantly telling a child he is Number One, besides predisposing him to failure, is that it convinces him he doesn't need anyone else, even God. As I mentioned in chapter fifteen, praise and encouragement help a child to succeed. But praise is strong medicine and like anything potent, it needs to be given out in measured doses. The only child often has the opposite problem of the youngest. The youngest child needs praise and encouragement while the only usually has an overdose. If a child is praised for every little thing he accomplishes, he is going to develop of spirit of pride and superiority. Also, since onlies never have to share the praise of their parents, they don't realize that others have this same need for encouragement.

What Paul said to the Philippians is especially relevant for the only child: "Do nothing out of selfish ambition or vain conceit, but in humility consider *others better than yourselves*. Each of you should look not only to your own interests, but also to the interests of others. Your attitude should be the same as that of

Christ Jesus . . ." (Philippians 2:3–5, NAS; italics mine). A child who is constantly being told that he is Number One is going to have a hard time counting others better, looking to the interests of others, and having the mind of Christ. Parents have to be careful not to make a child the only important thing in their lives. If all the family activities revolve around a child, he will soon come to feel he truly is the center of the universe. You can see how destructive this attitude would be to a Christian lifestyle. Parents must teach them that only Christ can be the best in life.

Bob's story may be a familiar one for many only males. Bob and his wife, Carol, have been in our fellowship for about twelve years. One night in our small house group, they discussed a problem they were having in their marriage. Carol said that Bob didn't seem to need her and after thirty years of marriage, they had no communication. "Bob comes home from work, eats dinner, and then does what he wants. He doesn't include me in his life."

Bob confessed that this was true. As an only child, he had learned to enjoy being alone and was quite content being with himself. I asked him if he believed he was born again. He answered that he had received Jesus as his Savior twelve years ago.

"But have you ever given Him your life?" I asked.

Bob said no, he hadn't really yielded up his life. Since Bob thought of himself as a superior person, as Number One, he could not relinquish control of his life. Bob felt convicted that night of his failure to yield his life totally to God.

We prayed with him and he asked Jesus to take the number one place in his life, to be not only his Savior but his Lord as well. The next week Carol happily reported that it was like living with a new person. Bob truly had the mind of Christ.

First children seem to have the hardest time yielding control of their lives to God because it is hard to admit they need help. Salvation is a transaction: God gives us His life and in exchange we give Him ours. The transaction isn't complete until we complete our part of the exchange.

One other thing about the male only child. It will also be hard for him to understand that other people are just as important to God as he is. He may be a special child, but God views all His children as special · The suggestions in chapter thirteen for teaching children to empathize with others would be helpful for the only child.

Female onlies also receive a lot of attention from their parents but in a more negative way. They are frequently reminded that they are not measuring up to the parents' expectations. They are perfectionistic in that they try to be complete and thorough in everything they undertake simply because they are prone to a sense of worthlessness whenever they are accused of not measuring up; the emphasis in this kind of perfectionism is on avoiding any kind of criticism.[7]

This results in adult onlies who crave approval and are vulnerable to criticism. I have observed that only women are prone to pettiness. They will continually rehash every little real or imagined slight that occurs to them. Because their parents gave them excessive attention in a critical way, they become consumed with everything that happens to them and have a hard time forgiving. They, too, need to become more concerned about other people than they are about themselves. In this way, the pettiness will disappear. One of the best ways to consider others more important is through serving. Only children are usually not servers since they were not called on to help with household tasks. Parents need to teach their only children the importance of serving others through their example and also by giving them different responsibilities.

One aspect of pettiness is that it is the negative side of a positive strength—that of being analytical. If only children can find a positive outlet for this strength, the negative side will not be a problem. Our fellowship gave the task of organizing all the children's Bible studies to Liz, an only child. Her attention to detail and her analytical manner make her an excellent organizer. Also, only children are the most reliable group of people and usually do what they say they will do when they say they will do it.[8]

Three Areas of Concern

Being an only child is like the "good news/bad news" joke. The good news is that the only child always has his parents to himself. The bad news is that his parents will expect him to fulfill every one of their desires, dreams, and ambitions. Dr. Kappelman feels that the overambition and overinvestment of the parents will fall into three areas: education, creativity, and athletics.[9] Here is an overview of each of these areas, and guardrails to help parents of the only child stay on the right track.

Education

A study of more than ten thousand children in Scotland provided the clear finding that only children scored higher on intelligence tests than did members of sibling groups. At age eleven, the average IQ score for only children was 105, and for children from large families, 90.[10]

Naturally, not every only child is brilliant. But if the parents of only children are well-educated, they may not expect their child to be anything but a budding genius. They may pressure the child to achieve beyond his level of ability. Like the first-born, this pressure will cause the only to be a compulsive overachiever or to be discouraged and give up completely. If the child accepts their standards he will drive himself to achieve. Often the child can keep up until college when the level of competition becomes more than he can handle. For this reason, "it is not unusual for the only child to go through periods of depression and loss of self-esteem and some consequent academic problems during his freshman year."[11]

Parents need to appraise their child's abilities realistically and not set goals beyond his capabilities. To tell a child, "You can be the best" is useless and frustrating if the child doesn't have the capability to achieve the best. As with the first child, parents have to be sure they don't direct their child down the educational corridors they themselves wanted to go.

Friends of ours with an only child began to direct him toward the field of medicine while he was in high school. He took a pre-med curriculum in college and received only average grades. This didn't deter the parents who continued to assure him this was the way to go. His grades on the medical entrance exam were about average but the parents continued to push him to apply to medical school. He did and was rejected, and probably felt he had failed completely. After looking at all his options, he decided to make a complete change of course and later obtained a Master's degree in the school of business. All's well that ends well, but if his parents had properly assessed his interests when he was younger, he would have been spared some very painful lessons.

The only child, like the youngest, is often given a lot of help and support by his parents in his schoolwork. One disadvantage "in relying on such help from supposedly stronger people, is that they never come to accept their own capabilities. No matter what the outside world says about his abilities, such an only child will retain an inner feeling that he could not have succeeded through his own efforts, and he will have little enjoyment of his success."[12] Parents need to be cautious abut giving too much help to the only with his schoolwork. Even though parents may have the time, the only needs to feel he is capable of doing his own work.

The first child of several, besides desiring the approval of his parents for his achievement, also desires to compete with his younger brothers and sisters. The only child does not have this added element of sibling competition, and will eventually ease up in his desire to achieve. Once he enters the working world, his chief motivation may be to "obtain the good things he can buy and the pleasant situations he can afford as a result of his efforts."[13] Actually, in the working world this relaxed attitude will be an advantage as fellow employees will feel comfortable around him and not competitive.

Creativity

A new book called *The Hurried Child* has alerted parents to the danger of overloading their children with activities. No child is in more danger of this happening than the only child. In multi-child families the parents are kept from involving their children in too many activities because of a lack of time and money. I can remember trying to juggle John's guitar lessons, Shannon's ballet classes, and Tom's trumpet lessons. Then there were Indian guides, Girl Scouts, Brownies (for Kelly), and assorted sports. The parents of an only have one child to spend their money on and to drive to lessons so it is easy to overload this child with too many activities.

Dr. Kappelman says that "one of the most creative gifts a parent can develop in his child is how to use free time."[14] Wilson and Edington, two clinical psychologists, feel that many onlies and first-borns are "Type A" persons.[15] Type A's have a chronic sense of time urgency and their life becomes a "hurry-up" kind of race. They are unable to relax without feeling guilty and leisure activities do not bring relaxation because they are overplanned or overscheduled. The Type A person needs to win and has an extreme desire for advancement and recognition. You can see how onlies and other first-borns fit this description and how the parents' push for achievement can aggravate this problem.

Cardiologists believe that the major cause of coronary artery and heart disease is a complex interweaving of emotional reactions that they have designated a Type A Behavior Pattern. One of the amazing findings is that "in the absence of Type A Behavior Pattern, coronary heart disease almost never occurs before seventy years of age, regardless of the fatty foods eaten, the cigarettes smoked, or the lack of exercise. But when this behavior pattern is present, coronary heart disease can easily erupt in one's thirties or forties."[16]

It is vital that Christian parents realize what achievement is all about, not only for the physical health of the child but also for his spiritual welfare. "What profit is there if you gain the whole world—and lose eternal life?" (Matthew 16:26, LB). Real achievement is fulfilling God's plan for our lives regardless of what we achieve. To turn our children into Type A persons whose only goal is to win and achieve worldly recognition is to fail at the task of parenting. Parents of onlies need to be sure that the child has free time to relax and enjoy being a child.

All four of my children still remember with fondness the summers we spent in our home by the lake. I tend to be a Type A person myself, but moving to the lake during the summer changed my personality. We lived unscheduled days and fully enjoyed our long lazy summers. Although my children had chores, most of the day was their own. They swam, water-skied, built sand castles; the girls played dolls, the boys G.I. Joes; they read, and sometimes just sat staring out the window. But there were no lessons, Little Leagues, classes, or schedules, and they could enjoy the fleeting irresponsibility of childhood. Even today all four of them still make good use of their free time. It even helped my oldest not be a workaholic. I thank God that He helped me let down on my hectic schedule at least for three months of the year and allow my kids to be kids.

Athletics

Athletics is another area where the adults may try to impose their wishes on the only child and push him into something for which he does not have the ability. In the 1974 issue of the United Nations publication *Development Forum*, the physical superiority of only children was well documented by Dr. E. James Lieberman.[17] There is a preponderance of only children in sports and in other rigorous occupations.

The only child, however, is not a team player. He has not had brothers and sisters to play with and he does not know how to submit his individual role for the good of the team. Only children are often drawn to sports that emphasize individual accomplishments. That way they can work on their own and receive individual attention.

Our friend Dave was the captain of the high school swim team and enjoyed the recognition for his achievement. He confessed to us he didn't like swimming relay because, if they won, he had to share the acclamation.

Encouraging the only child when he is young to engage in group sports would be a good way to help him learn teamwork. The only child always wants to be noticed and doesn't like being one of the many. Jesus said, "For whoever wishes to save his life shall lose it; but whoever loses his life for My sake shall find it" (Matthew 16:25, NAS). We can't be a Christian and always "save our life" by being first, being noticed, and being praised. We need to teach our only child that to achieve a common goal we often have to subjugate our need for recognition and our desires by being willing to "lose our life" for the benefit of others.

Dave is also a talented pianist but no one could take advantage of his talent in the past. Whenever he played with the worship band, his piano could be heard above all the other instruments. He put in just enough different notes so that, instead of blending, he was playing alone. Dave has had to give up his music temporarily. As he learns to serve others and die to the need to be first, I know God will once again give him the opportunity to play.

Parents of an only child walk a thin tightrope: They want their child to have a good self-image and to know he is special, but they do not want him to think he is better than other people or to go through life seeking recognition. Parents need to be careful not to make their child the only important thing in their lives. The structure of the family unit is vital to the child's well-being and in the next chapter we will discuss the dynamics of interaction in the one-child family.

Parenting Pointers

1. Because there is only one child, parents need to beware of indulging his every whim. Otherwise he will become a little dictator.

2. Domination by the parents is a danger for the quiet or passive child. Parents need to encourage their child to make his own decisions early in life and live with his errors.

3. Beware issuing too many warnings or instructions to your child or he will grow up timid and pessimistic.

4. Parents must practice consistent discipline with their only child and establish firm rules of behavior. Parents should recognize their lack of experience and study Christian books on discipline. It is important that the parents agree on the rules and present a united front.

5. Do not build up the child's sense of pride and superiority by urging him to be the best at everything but rather to imitate Christ who came not to be served but to serve (Matthew 20:28).

6. Be realistic in your assessment of your child's capabilities in education, athletics, and creative pursuits. Do not push him in directions you yourself wanted to pursue.

7. Do not overload your child with lessons and activities. Allow him unscheduled time.

8. Encourage your child to participate in team sports and activities whenever possible.

9. Be clear in your own mind about the true meaning of achievement in the Kingdom of God and impart this to your child.

Seventeen

The One-Child Family

The one-child family is by its nature intense. Three people living together in such close quarters are bound to experience problems especially if they look to each other to fulfill their needs. In a multi-child family there is more room for error because the children can provide needed emotional support for one another. If the parents are going through difficult times, the children can turn to each other for comfort. The only child has no other emotional supports.

Because of the small structure of the one-child family, it is imperative that the family be founded on biblical principles. This is particularly important in relation to the parents' God-given sexual roles if the child is to grow up secure in his or her own sexual role.

In fact, the parents' relationship is such an important factor in the only child's development that he can suffer serious effects from a consistently poor one. Research has shown that one of the extreme effects, and one that we will consider here, is homosexuality. "Several studies have revealed that a preponderance of homosexuals are either only children or come from two-child families."[1] A study done at Illinois State University found that two-thirds of a sample of 205 lesbians were only children.[2] Since the only child does not have brothers and sisters, it must be something in the parents' relationship that opens the child to homosexuality. Because the parents' role is so vitally important in the nurturing of children—particularly the only child—I'd like to focus here on what sometimes goes wrong in those roles, specifically as they relate to the child's sexual identity.

Absentee Father

The first has to do with the influence of the father. We are finding out today that "fathers have enormous influence on the sex-role identification of their children. Fathers seem to become a more salient role model to sons, while the mothers, for the most part, continue to give equal attention to children of both genders."[3] Two researchers after reviewing all the reports of male homosexuals concluded: "There is not a single even moderately well controlled study that we have been able to locate in which male homosexuals refer to father positively or affectionately. On the contrary, they consistently regard him as an antagonist."[4] The fathers of male homosexuals were described as "cold, unfriendly, punishing, brutal, distant, detached."

Much less research has been devoted to discovering the causes of female homosexuality. "However, there is a consistent train of findings . . . that the father of the female homosexual dealt with her in a frustrating, disappointing fashion."[5] "Without exception, these studies indicate that the female homosexual thinks of her father as an unfriendly, unpleasant person who had little to offer by way of a relationship."[6]

If a father is too preoccupied or disinclined to give his children the attention they need, then the boys do not have a strong role model to encourage their developing masculinity and the girls learn (usually from their mothers) that men are undependable or unnecessary. Adding to the identity problem in the one-child family, researchers found with small children that "only children tend to be more androgynous—exhibiting some of the characteristics that have been associated with both their own and the other sex."[7] On the other hand, "kindergarten children who have siblings are much more rigid about what is appropriate for boys and girls." Evidently having siblings, and especially sisters, seems to result in distinct and separate roles.

My husband and I work with drug addicts from the inner city of Chicago. Most are black and from a ghetto type of environment, and have grown up in a home without a father or with a father who was abusive or an addict himself. The males from this type of home are often jobless and turn to drugs as a relief from the boredom of life. Dr. Peter Blitchington found in his research that "in cultures where most men are missing from family units—and the families are headed by women—the children will be less disciplined, less industrious, and less productive than in cultures where fathers are in the home and working."[8]

The women from these inner-city homes are often prostitutes who harbor a deep hatred for men. Most have been betrayed by the close men in their lives—deserted by their fathers, abused by their brothers—and therefore have a hard time accepting their femininity. It is almost impossible for them to move into a loving and dependent relationship with God the Father (who is also a Man) without first healing those emotional wounds.

Just as God the Father gives us our identity through His Son Jesus Christ, so the earthly father has been given the task of providing his children with their identities. If the father fails in his role, his children may never find theirs. But if the father fills his provider role with energy and dignity he will pass the right values on to his children to help them in their own search for identity.

The Controlling Mother

The second mistake in parental roles has to do with the influence of the mother in light of the absentee or weak father. Sometimes, perhaps to compensate for the absence of the father, mothers make one of two huge errors: either they get too close to their children—particularly their sons—or grow hostile and domineering. Both are a type of control.

The Emotionally Dependent Mother

In the first case, if the mother of an only son is unhappy in her marital relationship, she may turn to the child for the emotional support she should be getting from her husband. But turning to a child for love and comfort places a terrible burden on him and, in the case of the only or oldest son, alienates him from his father. He thus becomes his father's rival for the mother and this makes it impossible to have a close relationship with the father. We must remember that God intended for the husband and wife to be a complement to one another, but that no one person can fulfill our every need. God is the only one who can have that role in our lives.

I entered married life with some very unrealistic expectations. I grew up in the '50s era when happy families and ideal marriages were portrayed daily on television, radio, and in magazines. I expected my husband to be able to meet every need and keep me from ever being depressed and unhappy. Even after I became a Christian I continued in this fantasy. As you can imagine, it caused quite a bit of conflict within our marriage. Every time I needed a scapegoat for my unhappiness, it was my husband; if he were doing a better job, I would surely be happier and more fulfilled.

One day while praying about a conflict that had occurred between us, I realized that only God could give me total fulfillment and happiness. Because He is a jealous God (Exodus 20:5),

He did not want anyone else to be able to take His place in my life. Once I realized that my fulfillment and happiness were dependent on God alone, our marriage underwent an amazing change. I didn't pressure my husband to meet my unrealistic expectations and, since he wasn't under my burden, he was freer to become the husband God intended.

We see in the story of Isaac and Rebekah a mother turning to one of her sons for the relationship she should have had with her husband. Rebekah favored Jacob, the younger twin—a Mama's boy who helped her in the kitchen. Isaac, on the other hand, preferred Esau who was a hunter and outdoorsman (Genesis 25).

Let's look at Isaac for a moment. He was, like his son Jacob, a Mama's boy. He was still grieving for his mother three years after her death (Genesis 24:67), which shows the tremendous bond between mother and son. Isaac probably saw his weaknesses mirrored in Jacob who was also attached to his mother and disliked him for it. Remember, too, Isaac was an only child. When he met his future wife, he was returning from a time of quiet meditation in the fields (Genesis 24:63). Only children continue to need times of solitude even in adulthood and this tendency to withdraw continues in the marriage relationship.

Whatever it was that caused Rebekah's lack of fulfillment in her marriage, she sought from Jacob what she lacked in her relationship with Isaac. It is evident that they had a relationship that excluded Isaac as they schemed together to steal Esau's blessing from his father (Genesis 27).

Mother and son had a relationship that should be reserved for the husband and wife. As a result, the whole family suffered loss: Esau lost his birthright, Isaac and Rebekah lost the relationship God intended them to have, and Jacob lost his home when he had to flee Esau's wrath. Rebekah was the big loser, though: She ended up losing all her relationships. Ultimately, perversion of God's order will always bring loss and heartbreak.

If we have done this in marriage, we need to repent and ask God's forgiveness. I have found it easier to repent when I call sin by its real name and don't try to sugarcoat it. If you have looked to your son to give you the emotional support you should have received from your husband, it is a form of incest! Confessing it as such and releasing the bondage you have placed over your son will help to set him free from the effects. It might also be good to ask your husband's forgiveness for seeking a relationship with your son that you should have looked for in him.

The Domineering Mother

The other mistake mothers make toward an only child is to become domineering and overbearing. Instead of becoming emotionally dependent on her son or daughter, she dominates, overprotects, and controls.

Dr. David Levy in *Maternal Overprotection*[9] outlines four types of behavior most often found in domineering mothers:

1. Excessive contact: One example would be allowing the child to continue to sleep in the bed with the mother into his teens. An acquaintance of ours was dying of cancer in the hospital. His wife allowed their fourteen year old son to sleep with her at night during this time. The mother and son were angry and confused because of the impending death of the husband and so sought comfort in one another. This type of situation has certainly pre-conditioned the boy to incest or homosexuality. No matter what the situation, mothers need to be able to tolerate their own grief, loneliness, or pain and not use their child as an answer to their problem. Otherwise the mother is sacrificing her child to her own selfishness.

2. Infantilization: Babying the child by doing things for him that he should be doing himself such as continuing to dress him when he is old enough to dress himself. I have seen mothers continue to feed their children when they should have been feeding themselves simply to avoid the mess a child makes when he tries to eat by himself.

3. Prevention of independent behavior: Not allow the child to

walk to school alone when his peers do, for instance. With only one child it is so easy to drive that child anywhere he has to go. Instead of being grateful to Mother for all the things she did for him, the dependent child will come to dislike her for making him weak and dependent. The mother in turn will dislike the child for being so dependent and weak.

4. Lack or excess of maternal control: As we mentioned in the last chapter, this results in overindulgence and letting the child do whatever he wants or controlling him by an elaborate set of rules.

Levy found that these mothers had an unsatisfied desire for love that was not fulfilled in their childhood. They may have had difficulties with conception or lost other children at birth or infancy. Also there was sexual maladjustment in the marriage and a lack of outside social contacts.

The Loneliness Factor

But even in happy homes with solid parental relationships, parents can't fulfill all the needs of the child. Even the best of parents cannot "provide the social intercourse so necessary for the unfolding of a growing child's emotional life."[10] No matter how hard parents of an only child try to fill his life with companionship and friends, he will still spend more time alone than a child with brothers and sisters. And because children see things differently from adults, the things that are important to a child may not be important to an adult. A child may be fascinated by an ant carrying a crumb of bread and want to discuss this wonderful observation with a parent who sees the ant only as a household pest. Brothers and sisters can share in each other's world and events keep their importance. An only child will feel this lack.

My sister's daughter, Lisa, who was an only child for nine years, used to get up Christmas morning, open her gifts, and immediately call our home to talk to John, Shannon, and Tom. She could hardly wait to discuss her presents with my children.

Parents are just not able to share the excitement of special moments with their children in the same way. We are too far removed from the world of the child to appreciate them.

Dr. Kappelman cautions parents of an only child to be acutely aware of this difference. He goes on to say that this awareness will enable parents to be good listeners without offering a lot of advice.[11] Sometimes we just need to be able to listen to our children and try to enter into their excitement and see things the way they see them. We have to beware of always adding our comments, warnings, or opinions or soon they will stop sharing with us.

There are times when the only child is especially isolated such as evenings, weekends, and summers. These periods of loneliness can be eased by inviting other children over to play.

Fantasy World

Because of so much alone time, the only child often creates a fantasy world. Although all children spend some time fantasizing, brothers and sisters force each other to keep in touch with reality. The only child is able to indulge himself in his dreams and fantasies without worrying about too much interruption.

Most children between the ages of two and four create some type of fantasy world and parents need not be too concerned. However, "when the only child creates an imaginary sibling rather than an imaginary friend or pet, the parents should thoroughly and sensitively examine their relationship with their child."[12] This may be a signal that the child is uncomfortable with the intense attention of his parents and desires a brother or sister to absorb some of it. If the parents have a close relationship with each other and are involved in activities outside the home, they will probably not err in focusing too much attention on their child. If their child is the only important thing in their lives, however, they are in for some future problems.

Other problems might be inherent in the type of fantasy friend the child invents. Jana was about three when her little baby brother was born. Soon after her little brother came home from the hospital, Jana began to talk with a new friend named Tony. Sometimes Jana said Tony would try to hurt her and she would roll around on the floor and cry for her mother to make Tony go away. Jana was acting out her feelings toward her new baby brother and the displacement she felt through Tony.

Her mother came to see me to discuss Jana's fantasy friend. Teri was also a first-born girl and she recalled feeling that she was a disappointment to her parents.

"I know they wanted a boy," said Teri, "and because of that I could never accept my femininity. Do you think I passed that same feeling on to my first-born daughter?"

We found that Teri had indeed passed this on to her daughter. She was able to pray and forgive her mother and father for the rejection she felt growing up. Then she asked God's forgiveness for doing the same thing to her daughter. That night Teri talked to Jana and reassured her that she was so happy she was a little girl. She talked of all the things mother and daughters could do together and the fun they would have.

As Jana snuggled under her covers that night she told her mother she had a new friend. The name of her new friend was Lisa. Teri knew this girl fantasy friend symbolized a feeling of security and acceptance. The new friend was short-lived and within a week she, too, disappeared.

Dr. Kappelman warns parents that, although they may let the child know they are aware of the imaginary friend, they must never let the friend become part of the family's reality. Children are unable to mix fantasy and reality. Setting a place at the table for the imaginary playmate, talking to it, or in any other way acknowledging its existence, would be harmful to the child and reinforce the fantasy.

Creative Solitude

Being alone does not only have negative connotations but positive as well. Younger children in the family who always have people around may become adults who are not comfortable being alone. The only children at our meeting all reinforced the idea that they liked being alone and that they used their alone time productively. This accounts for the self-sufficiency of most only children.

One man, Virgil, said that being alone so much forced him to learn things on his own whether it was the assembly of a toy or the directions of a board game. This is a distinct advantage and probably accounts for the school success of only children. Only children have a lot of creative solitude, which gives them a richness of imagination and innovation. [13]

It is my opinion that only children, like first-borns, would make good teachers of the Word. A teacher has to be able to tolerate loneliness while he studies and researches the Bible. Most teachers are not people persons but rather idea persons and this is descriptive of the only child and other first-borns. Also, a teacher has to be sensitive to details and organization—two skills at which only children excel. One researcher says that only children derive solid and deep satisfaction from immersing themselves in whatever they undertake until they are an authority on whatever has captured their attention. [14] This is a description of the ministry of teaching.

Friends and the Only Child

In our discussion of loneliness among only children, Liz mentioned that she was not lonely when she was alone but rather "lonely in a crowd." It was then that her "onliness" really stood out. In a family setting the child learns most about relationships. A child with brothers and sisters learns to take for granted the interplay of emotions and the behavior swings of brothers and sisters.

Virgil mentioned that he cannot understand his two daughters. "They can be tearing each other's hair out one minute and buddies the next. I don't understand how they can forgive so easily." Virgil then went on to say that he often carried grudges for a long time against people who hurt him.

This inability to understand relationships is one of the biggest drawbacks to growing up an only child. Brothers and sisters don't get too disturbed about arguments and know that the same sibling you hate today may be your best friend tomorrow. Siblings learn to work out their own problems with one another—one day the power may be in your favor and the next day you may have to give in. In this way they learn the skills of negotiation.

The only child bargains with the adult world where there are different skills. Also, the only child is always dealing with two adults who are bigger, stronger, and smarter. This gives the child a feeling of always being weaker in relationships. To compensate for this insecurity, the only children interviewed said they liked relationships where they were in control. Most admitted they were drawn to friends who liked to talk about themselves but didn't demand the same of them.

The only child is insecure in relationships and hides his insecurity behind a mask of congeniality. Having grown up in an adult world they are great at small talk and saying the right thing at the right time. The only child may appear sophisticated and adult but usually feels on the outside of any group gathering. Karl König says that the only child "stands in the doorway, he is neither in nor out, he is almost always at the threshold."[15] "He is kept away from his immediate social environment. He views it from within the gate of his own house and around him the world is strange yet known. He takes part in the activities of the world without really partaking."[16]

This is an accurate description of the only child. Our group shed some further light on this problem. Only children do not feel a part of things but they also don't want to break into the group. This is because they do not want to expose themselves and relationships bring exposure. Virgil said he was so private about his life that he instructed his wife she was never to talk about him with her friends. "I didn't even want anyone to know what brand of toothpaste I used," he told us.

Because only children grow up without siblings, they fantasize about what it would be like to have a sibling. Their fantasies don't include real-life situations like jealousy and competition but are idealized relationships. Unfortunately, only children project these high standards onto their friendships and expect their friends to have all these ideal qualities. The only child counts on a great deal from friends in the way of attention and companionship. He is used to only considering his plans and wishes and expects his friends to do the same. These unrealistic expectations will destroy a friendship and the only child will be left hurt and bewildered but no wiser.

Lisa told us that she was always having some crisis with her friends; Dave said it was a feeling of friends constantly failing him that almost caused him to leave the fellowship the year before. This problem of unrealistic expectations will not only cause ruined friendships but will undermine the spiritual growth of the person. It is relationships that force us to grow and change. If we are afraid of relationships or getting hurt by people, we will never learn to look at ourselves and our need to change.

One of the biggest problems for the only child is accepting people as they are instead of projecting expectations onto them. Parents need to work harder with an only child to encourage the child to find outside friends. Then parents can help the child when he goes through difficulties in his friendship by helping him understand the other child's point of view. If Mother always defends her child, she is simply reinforcing his aloneness. Making new friendships is important, first, for the child to learn the give and take of group experiences. Remember that the only child never has to share at home with his parents so it is important that he learn by playing with others.

My sister, Jeannie, brought her only daughter over to our house at least two or three times a week to play. Lisa soon learned to fit into the group. She also did her fair share of bossing, arguing, and making up. In this way Lisa learned the give and take of sibling relationships and later social relationships. Parents especially need to put extra effort into exposing their only child to other children and group activities before the age of five. If kindergarten is the first time the only child is involved in a group activity, it will be difficult to adjust. Camp, scouting, and church activities can all provide needed companionship and training in relationships.

Only children should develop friendships for a second reason, one that may be difficult for some parents to accept: The child simply needs to spend time away from the parents.

There are two main reasons why parents of onlies have trouble letting go. The authors of *The Only Child* have found that the principal reason is the "fear that the child will be accidentally killed or injured."[17] If you have that hidden fear for your child you need to confess and release it to God. Satan can attack us on the basis of fear but once it is confessed and given to God, he has no more ground over us.

The other reason parents don't give this child more independence is that often they want to control all aspects of their child's life so he will become the "perfect" child. If they allow him a life away from them with other children, they will lose that control.

More than any other birth order, only children have the hardest time breaking close ties with their parents. The parents of an only child need to realize that if they succeed at their parenting task, they will train the child to be independent of them. That means practicing releasing the child from the time he is small. The best safeguard against a mutual overdependence is that the parents have a good relationship and are putting the Kingdom of God first in their lives. The parents should have outside activities that do not include the child so the only knows that they have a life apart from him. This also releases the child from the pressure of being all things to his parents. Parents who want to raise a successful only child need first to love and prefer each other above the child and to be working together in the Kingdom of God. Then the child will grow up with the proper perspective of his place in the family.

Parenting Pointers

1. The father needs to understand the supreme importance of his role in the home to provide the sexual identity for his children. He should take time to invest himself in the life of his child to ensure a good relationship.

2. The mother needs to beware forming too close an association with her son. He should not become the companion of the mother.

3. The mother must avoid becoming domineering or controlling through (1) excessive contact, (2) infantilization, (3) prevention of independent behavior, and (4) lack or excess of maternal control.

4. The mother needs to check her attitudes about men. If she has unforgiveness toward a male figure she may well pass these negative attitudes on to a son or daughter. The son would learn to despise his masculinity and the daughter would learn to reject men.

5. Parents of an only child need to make an extra effort to provide their child with play partners and group activities.

6. The only child often has fantasy friends and the nature of the friend may signal a problem. Never allow the fantasy friend to have any reality in the family.

7. Help your child to develop a realistic understanding of friendships and allow him to settle his own conflicts.

8. Practice releasing your child by allowing him to participate in outside activities and overnight trips.

9. Realize that to raise a secure child the parents must be secure in their relationship with each other and in their relationship with God.

Eighteen

Mirror, Mirror

God's intention in giving us children was that they would be a blessing to us (Psalm 127:3). As a parent myself, I know that there have been times when I have doubted the truth of that particular Scripture verse. My emotions concerning my children can range from a tremendous sense of pride to utter despair—sometimes within the same day. Over the years I have learned that even in those times of despair our children are still a blessing to us. Since our children are extensions of ourselves, they reflect both our good and bad qualities. God uses our children to reveal our (1) sins, (2) hidden attitudes, and (3) power struggles. I would like to use the story of Tom's struggle with drugs to show how even our darkest times with our children can be turned, by the hand of God, into a blessing for both parents.

Sins

Most of us are familiar with the story of Elijah who prophesied to the wicked King Ahab that there would be no rain or dew for three years. Ahab was furious and sought to kill Elijah so God sent him to stay with a widow and her only son. While he was staying in her house, her son died and she made a very revealing statement: "What do I have to do with you, O man of God? You have come to me to *bring my iniquity to remembrance*, and to put my son to death!" (1 Kings 17:18, NAS; italics mine).

Somehow she connected her son's death with some sin in her past life. It was almost as if the guilt of her sin was always there waiting, expecting punishment, and now it had come. The New Testament would explain it by the verse that says, "For whatever a man sows, this he will also reap" (Galatians 6:7, NAS). But God's purpose for the widow and for each one of us when he brings our sin to remembrance through our children is for healing and not for destruction. Elijah prayed for her son and God restored him to life. As a result, the woman had a new faith in God and in the prophet.

Similarly, with Tom, God used a traumatic event to reveal a hidden sin and judgment in the life of his father. Tom is the third-born son of a third-born son—John—of a third-born— Grandad. Grandad, like Tom and John, followed an achieving first-born and a "saintly" second-born. As he looked around for an identity, he chose to be a rebel and often boasted to us that he was the black sheep of the family of seven children. My husband, while not a rebel, was definitely an underachiever. He drifted from one college to another, flunking several courses. After about four different colleges and a two-year stint in the Army, he finally settled down and, by some miracle, was accepted into dental school. This was the turning point for him—he did well in school and was even elected president of the student body organization. But this black-sheep pattern continued into the third generation. Tom, also following an achieving first-born and an agreeable second-born (her little sister calls her "angel child"), became a classic underachiever. He was the class clown through many school years and seemed to be the one child who was always getting into some kind of mischief. I also found out through his little sister Kelly (the family informant) that he, too, called himself the black sheep of the family and certainly his actions demonstrated he was trying to bring to pass this self-fulfilling prophecy.

Several nights after Tom confessed his drug addiction, we met for prayer with some of the leaders in our fellowship. As we were praying, John was reminded of a judgment he had placed upon his father. John never had a close relationship with his father, who worked hard to provide for the family but had absolutely no involvement with the children. John judged him to be a poor father and felt unforgiveness, resentment, and rejection from him. He was unaware of these attitudes until the Holy Spirit revealed them as we prayed. That night he asked God's forgiveness for his bitterness and forgave his father. He also released him from his judgment. Scripture warns us: "Do not judge lest you be judged. For in the way you judge, you will be judged; and by your standard of measure, it will be measured to you" (Matthew 7:1–2, NAS).

John had judged his father and his judgment was coming back to us through our son Tom. In fact, we had often laughed about things we saw in Tom when he was growing up, saying, "Well, he's just like Grandad." We were binding Tom by our judgment so that he, too, saw himself, like Grandad, as the black sheep. God in His mercy used our son's addiction to remind John of his past sin—not to condemn and destroy him—rather to allow him to confess it and set both Grandad and Tom free of that judgment. This was the first step in setting my son free from his drug addiction and the second was to involve me.

Hidden Attitudes

The day after I found out about Tom's drug problem, I had a wonderful time of praise and fellowship with God. I spent the morning praying, reading my Bible, and singing songs of praise to God for the victory I knew that He would accomplish. I even remember thinking how spiritual I had become that even this problem didn't interupt my fellowship with God.

As the weeks passed and Tom was still struggling and only having limited success in overcoming the temptation to take cocaine, I found my enthusiastic praise choruses growing fewer and farther between. Finally, I had to admit to myself that there was blockage in my prayer life.

About that time the mother of an old friend died and we made the hour's drive to attend the wake. Jerry and his wife had been our closest friends all during and after dental school. We went through the hard times and the good times together—until John and I became Christians. Then we had a parting of the ways. Jerry even told us the reason: He wanted to make a lot of money and didn't have time for Christianity even though he readily acknowledged the peace and happiness it brought into our lives.

This would be the first time we had seen them in years. Their oldest son was home from college for the funeral and we were both surprised and amused to discover that he was a committed Christian. Amused because we knew of his father's decision to pursue money over God. Now his son had decided to forgo medical school (his father's desire for him) and go to the mission field. This man who said no to God had a son who said yes.

The next day as I was out jogging I was aware of an uncomfortable feeling in the middle of my chest. It was almost as if something was building inside me and demanding release. As I was running, I telegraphed a quick prayer to God to show me what I was keeping inside. Before my next foot hit the ground I knew. Anger! Anger so violent and so real it filled my eyes with tears and brought me to a standstill. I also realized the anger had been there a long time but had just been given specific words at the wake the night before. The bottom line was that for the last fourteen years my husband and I had tried as best we could to serve God, and we had a son on drugs. In contrast, there were our former friends who snubbed their noses at God, and they had a child who was committed to serving Him. It wasn't fair!

I was angry. So angry that I couldn't pray or read my Bible for several days. God had revealed a hidden attitude of my heart that I didn't know was there—and He did it through my son's problem. I somehow believed that God owed me something because I was serving Him. I would have denied that vehemently the week before but I knew now that it was true. I just didn't know what to do about it.

As my anger subsided I realized that I needed to get this area right with God. That meant setting aside a time to talk with Him. Somewhat reluctantly I decided that I would spend the next morning in a quiet time with God.

The next day as I sat there praying and meditating I realized that part of my anger was at myself. I certainly was not as spiritual as I imagined myself to be if I carried such a wrong attitude. I was even beginning to thank God for bringing out such a hidden but evil assumption. The more I thought about it the more repentant I became. Finally I could confess that God didn't owe me anything. The salvation He had given me as a gift was so far beyond what I deserved that to expect anything else was ludicrous. The next step was to totally release Tom. As I released him I prayed: "God, You don't owe me anything, even the salvation of my son. I release him to You to do as You see fit. It will not affect my love for or relationship with You and I will continue to serve You as long as You allow." It was frightening to release Tom not knowing what the outcome would be, but I felt a great peace in my soul.

Three days later Tom also had a confrontation with the living God. While praying for forgiveness because he had taken cocaine that night, he felt the love and forgiveness of God cleanse and heal him. For the first time he knew the reality of God's love.

That night Tom was completely and miraculously delivered from his addiction to cocaine. I often wonder if God had not given me the grace to deal with my hidden attitude how different the outcome might have been.

Power Struggle

The book *Breaking Points*, as I have mentioned, is a remarkably insightful book into the forces behind John Hinckley's assassination attempt on President Reagan. John was the third and youngest child in his family, following a successful older brother and a sister who was socially and intellectually superior. John was the "baby" and came to represent the power struggle between the parents. The mother was a fearful, overprotective person who wanted to baby and shield John while the father was success-oriented and tried to pressure John into achieving like the other children.

John wasn't the real problem, though. The real problem, which is replayed in practically every family, was "who was going to be the head of the home." John's parents, like most of us, admit they did not fight directly but rather chose John as the battleground. Very often, one child in the family becomes the vehicle through which the parents discharge their anger at one another and the trophy in that all-important battle for headship. It may be that the child is the baby of the family and especially attached to the mother, or perhaps the only one of that sex in the family and both parents are fighting for control. Whatever the reason, that child becomes the symbol of the "power struggle" that exists between the parents and, as always when there is such a struggle, the child is the ultimate loser. Put in the middle of the battle-field, with bullets flying at him from both sides, and each trying to win him over, the child becomes impotent. He is unable to make decisions and even to show love to one parent for fear of offending the other. Therefore, he has to repress his emotions and try to remain neutral. He has to separate his thoughts from his feelings to remain objective. These conditions may set the stage for a tendency to schizophrenia, which literally means two minds.

As I read the story of John Hinckley, I could see this power struggle between his parents. What I did not see at first was the similarity to my own marriage. Although I had come a long way in restoring the decision-making power to my husband, there was still a blind spot that I could not see until the Lord revealed it to me.

After Tom's deliverance from cocaine, he stayed clear from all drugs for a year-and-a-half. During that time, he learned to discipline his life both in physical exercise and by studying. He brought his low grade point up to a B and I breathed a sigh of relief that our troubles with Tom were over.

The summer between his junior and senior years of college started out badly and was a portent of things to come. He had planned to go out to the Boston area for the summer and work. He had a good job awaiting him and he was intent on proving he could make the break from home and survive. He told all his friends about his summer plans and left with the car filled with clothes, sports equipment, and farewell gifts.

The next we heard, he was stranded in Ohio and his car was not repairable. The young man who had left so full of enthusiasm and excitement returned dejected, in an ancient tow truck, with his "dead" car being dragged behind. For several days he wouldn't leave the house and certainly didn't want any of his friends knowing he was home.

Things went from bad to worse. He couldn't find a job since most of the college students had taken the available ones; he had no car; he and his girlfriend had parted ways. The inevitable phone call came about one A.M. a week later from Tom's best friend. He was worried about Tom because he had been drinking and taking Valium—a sometimes fatal combination. Was Tom home yet? Had we heard anything? A quick check of his room revealed he had not come home. The rest of the night we tossed and turned and prayed till we heard Tom's key in the lock about five A.M. My husband, who is a very wise man, suggested we wait till the next evening at dinner to talk to Tom.

During that long night, the Lord reminded me of how often I had protected Tom from his father. Maybe because he had been my baby for four years before his little sister was born or because I had guilt because of my early rejection of him, but for whatever reason, he was often in the middle between his father and me. I could not face the thought of another bout of drugs and the ensuing anxiety and worry. That night, as I lay in the darkness, I again released Tom—but this time to his father. I asked God to work through John, and said I would support him no matter how much I wanted to protect Tom.

The next night after dinner John told Tom he wanted to talk to him. Tom balked at the idea but my husband told him firmly he had no choice. I was surprised at the authority John displayed since he is a soft-spoken man. He then told Tom he was not going to underwrite his lifestyle and that he was either going to live by our rules or leave. Tom left home for three days after that confrontation and although I had no idea where he was, I had a peace in my heart that God was in control.

At the end of three days, Tom came home with a different spirit. He said he really wanted to get his life right and had no desire to resort to drugs again. It was then he asked if he could take a year off from school to join Youth With A Mission. My husband agreed and Tom went to Texas for the first part of his training. He received tremendous healing through the application of the Word of God and many of the attitudes that predisposed him to drug use were removed. It was an important time of healing for him, and I felt grateful that I had learned through my son to trust my husband fully as the spiritual head of our home.

I have come to see, in the fifteen years that my husband and I have been involved in pastoring a fellowship, how frequently God uses our children to "act out" a hidden attitude in us or to relive an incident we have not released from our past.

Recently, for instance, one of the couples in our fellowship was having a problem with their seven-year-old son who was stealing from the local drugstore. His parents are committed Christians and were completely baffled by their son's behavior. In their house church discussion, they realized that the father was unknowingly setting the example by "stealing" from his employer. Of course he didn't think it was stealing—he was only taking small office supplies. The parallel became obvious and when the father stopped his "stealing," the son's problem ceased likewise.

The book *The Long Way Home*[1] is John Jewell's story of his loss of faith and subsequent journey "into the far country" and finally, his return. I thought it quite revealing that during the time John Jewell was running away from God, his oldest son was actually running away from home. After John returned to his faith, his son was also restored. A coincidence? I don't think so. We can fool other people and we can even fool ourselves, but we eventually have to face what we are through our children. They are God's mirrors in our lives and often compel us to take a good look at ourselves.

I have nothing but thankfulness to God for this problem with Tom. There were many wrong attitudes and sins in his parents' lives that would have kept us from growing in God. Tom is a blessing to us now, but he has also been a blessing through his troubles. It forced us to face issues that would have been so easy to bury and ignore. God always intends our children to be a blessing; we just need to have a broader definition of what the word blessing means.

Nineteen

And, Finally

The hardest thing parents will ever do is to release their children totally to the will of God. It is not accomplished in one gigantic leap but rather in small, measured steps as the children walk into maturity. It's amazing how parents feel an omnipotent control over the lives of their children until something out of the ordinary occurs—illness, the first day of school, an accident, a camping experience—and suddenly they realize that they have to ask God's help and protection. Each of these occasions is an opportunity to release the child to God and is a rehearsal for that final release into adulthood. I am a "doer" and so I have learned to appreciate the times when I can do nothing in a situation. Then I know the power of God is activated. I didn't always feel that way. It took me years to understand the principle of accepting and releasing. . . .

During my high school years I had but one goal: to be a

cheerleader. All my energies were directed toward obtaining that coveted prize; it was the ultimate acceptance. Two times I came within a hair's-breadth of achieving my goal but both times unusual circumstances prevented my claiming the reward. My graduation was tinged with sadness. It didn't matter that I was in the National Honor Society, Vice Preident of the senior class, vice president of the Senior Girls Council, and active in the student government—I was a failure.

I didn't realize that disappointment had tunneled deep within my spirit like a burr, persistently reminding me that I had failed. Then I had a daughter. A blonde, blue-eyed daughter who was well-coordinated. She had the ability to become a cheerleader and, in doing so, would vindicate me. Shannon, however, had different ideas. She did not have the least desire to be a cheerleader; she was a quiet girl who had no wish to be the center of attention by jumping up and down and screaming out school chants.

Naturally, I was disappointed. But I still had another daughter who was the opposite of Shannon, not only in coloring, but Kelly had an outgoing personality. As she sang around the house into her toy "Mr. Microphone," I smiled, picturing her yelling into a megaphone at football games.

She also proved to be a disappointment since she directed her energy into the high school newspaper. (I should have seen the writing on the wall when she was young. She earned the nickname the "neighborhood newspaper" because of her candid reports to the neighbors of everything—and I do mean everything— that went on at home. How was I to know the name would be prophetic?)

Now all this disappointment in my daughters went on at a subconscious level. On the surface I was proud and happy with their accomplishments. I would never have believed that I was the type of mother who would try to fulfill her dreams and desires through her daughters. That was unthinkable! I was a dedicated Christian who wanted only God's will for my children's lives.

The first inkling I had that there was an unseen bondage was my inability to release Shannon to the Lord. I prayed and prayed but always knew that I had not released her even after she left home for college. One day while I was praying about this problem, that still, small voice of God spoke to me through my thoughts: *You cannot release Shannon because you have never accepted her exactly as I made her.*

That rubbed the burr of disappointment into my spirit and I realized it was true. It wasn't only that I wanted her to be a cheerleader; there were other ways that I wanted to change her— little helpful ways, I was sure. I knew what was best for her; after all, I was her mother. But, if we have never accepted the child God gives us, exactly as she is with all her weaknesses and strengths, then we can never give that child back to God. How can we release what we have never accepted? Or, how can we release what we have accepted conditionally?

Jesus said, "You shall know the truth and the truth shall make you free" (John 8:32, NAS). In that moment of knowing I asked God's forgiveness for attempting to change my daughter into what I thought she should be rather than accepting her just as she was and letting Him direct her life. I knew then that I had truly released Shannon.

Eventually God directed Shannon into law school. This was something I never imagined would be His plan for her life. Her father first suggested she take the Law School Entrance Exam during her senior year of college. I remember thinking when he suggested that, *Boy, is he wrong this time.* I was the one who was wrong! Shannon scored so well that she was offered a full scholarship. God has His plans for our children's lives but He cannot put His plan into action until we release our control. The catch is that we cannot release our control until we totally accept our child.

Using this knowledge I also began to pray to accept Kelly just as she was, not as I wanted her to be. I confessed that I didn't know God's plan for her life but I gave Him full control to lead her in the direction that would bring Him the most glory. Kelly's release wasn't final until she, too, left home for college. Then I yielded the responsibility for her life to God.

One painful realization during my twenty-five years of child rearing has been my inability to be the perfect parent. Even though I made it a priority and gave it my Type A all, I still fell short of the mark. It is this realization of my shortcomings that has led me to release my children to God who is able to use His power in my weakness (2 Corinthians 12:9). No wonder Paul went on to say, "Now I am glad to boast about how weak I am; I am glad to be a living demonstration of Christ's power, instead of showing off my own power and abilities" (LB). Like Paul, I will not boast about my abilities and talents as a parent but about a God who loves me enough to cover my mistakes and somehow make everything come out right. He is a God, after all, who rewards faith, not perfect lives. The best reward of all was drawing the children to Himself.

Not too long ago I was listening to music by the Christian group the Imperials. As I hummed along with the lively beat of "Old Buddha," I remembered a concert they gave in our town some years ago. I "dragged" a reluctant teenage son to hear them. I confess I spent most of the concert gazing out of the corner of my eye to see his reaction. Would this be the thing that would finally "turn him on to God"?

I started to chuckle as I remembered similar incidents over the years with my four children. There were the special speakers, musical groups, children's ministries, Gospel magicians, Bible weeks, and so on *ad infinitum*. And always, there was the hope in me that this would be the time fire would fall from heaven, my rebellious teenager would be convicted, and I could breathe a long, slow sigh of relief.

It never happened that way. God seems to take a special delight in confounding us scheming, controlling mothers who try to tell Him how to run His universe and, especially, our children's lives.

The fire did fall, but never in my way or in my timing. God maintained His sovereignty in spite of my insistent nagging demands. I learned, much to my chagrin, that He did get the job done and in ways both unexpected and perfectly suited to each child's personality.

As we understand the differences in our children and their needs, perhaps we can be more at ease about releasing them to their heavenly Father who knows best how to build their character. Then, once we have grasped the extent of His love for our children, we can concentrate on being co-workers with God rather than supervisor. For though we both desire the same results for our children, only He has the blueprints.

References

REFERENCES FOR CHAPTER 1

1. Ross Campbell, M.D., *How To Really Love Your Teenager*, (Wheaton, Ill.: Victor Books, 1981), p. 10.

REFERENCES FOR CHAPTER 2

1. John F. McDermott, Jr., M. D., *Raising Cain (& Abel Too)*, (New York: Wyden Books, distributed by Harper & Row, 1980), p. 7.
2. April Olzak, "Teen Suicide and the North Shore Connection," *Chicago Tribune Magazine* (July 27, 1980), pp. 13–21.
3. L. W. Hoffman, "The Father's Role in the Family and the Child's Peer-Group Adjustment," *Merrill-Palmer Quarterly*, 7 (1961), pp. 97–105.

REFERENCES FOR CHAPTER 3

1. McDermott, p. 16.
2. Ann Crittenden, "Babies Are Born Different," *McCall's* (September, 1986), pp. 107, 149, 150–151.
3. McDermott, p. 82.
4. Heinz L. Ansbacher and Rowena Ansbacher, *The Individual Psychology of Alfred Adler* (New York: Harper & Row, 1956), p. 376.

REFERENCES FOR CHAPTER 4

1. Bradford Wilson and George Edington, *First Child, Second Child* . . . (New York: McGraw-Hill Book Company, 1981), p. 215.
2. Lucille K. Forer, *Birth Order and Life Roles* (Springfield, Ill.: Charles C. Thomas, Publisher, 1969), p. 57.
3. Karl König, *Brothers and Sisters* (Blauvelt, N.Y.: St. George Books, 1963), p. 47.
4. Edith G. Neisser, *The Eldest Child* (New York: Harper & Row, Publishers, Inc., 1957), pp. 94–95.
5. König, p. 42.
6. Rudolf Dreikurs, *Children: The Challenge* (New York: E. P. Dutton, Inc., 1964), p. 30.
7. Marion Long, "First Sons," *Chicago Sun Times*, Family Weekly (July 22, 1984), p. 14.
8. Karl A. Olsson, *Come to the Party* (Waco, Tex.: Word Books, 1972), p. 162.
9. Campbell, pp. 122–123.
10. Neisser, p. 95.

REFERENCES FOR CHAPTER 5

1. Phyllis Bottome, *Alfred Adler, A Biography* (New York: G. P. Putnam's Sons, 1939), p. 151.
2. Neisser, p. 46.
3. Wilson and Edington, p. 61.
4. Walter Toman, *Family Constellation* (New York: Springer Publishing Company, Third Edition, 1976), p. 32.
5. Toman, p. 32.
6. Toman, p. 33.
7. Joan Solomon Weiss, *Your Second Child* (New York: Summit Books, 1981), p. 96.
8. Ansbacher and Ansbacher, p. 378.

9. Neisser, p. 55.
10. Dreikurs, *Children: The Challenge*, p. 34.
11. Wilson and Edington, p. 80.

REFERENCES FOR CHAPTER 6

1. Joan Kalhorn Lasko, "Parent Behavior Toward First and Second Children," *Genetic Psychology Monographs*, 49 (1954), pp. 96–137.
2. Lawrence Kayton and George F. Borge, "Birth-Order and the Obsessive Compulsive Character," *Arch. Gen Psychial*, 17 (1967), pp. 751–754.
3. König, p. 43.
4. Ezra Stotland, Stanley E. Sherman, and Kelly G. Shaver, *Empathy and Birth-Order: Some Experimental Explorations* (Lincoln, Nebraska: U. of Nebraska Press, 1971), pp. 50–51.
5. Neisser, p. 123.
6. John Powell, *Why Am I Afraid to Love?* (Allen, Tex.: Tabor Publishing, 1967), pp. 95–96.
7. Stotland, Sherman, and Shaver, p. 51.
8. Forer, *Birth Order and Life Roles*, p. 100.

REFERENCES FOR CHAPTER 7

1. Weiss, p. 59.
2. Weiss, pp. 17–18.
3. Judy Dunn and Carol Kendrick, "The Arrival of a Sibling: Changes in Patterns of Interaction Between Mother and First-Born Child," *J. Child Psychol. Psychiat.*, 21, (1980), pp. 119–132.
4. Weiss, p. 184.
5. Weiss, p. 162.
6. Blanche S. Jacobs and Howard A. Moss, "Birth Order and

Sex of Sibling as Determinants of Mother-Infant Interaction," *Child Development*, 47 (1976), pp. 315–322.
7. Michael Lewis and Valerie S. Kreitzberg, "Effects of Birth Order and Spacing on Mother-Infant Interactions," *Developmental Psychology*, 15, No. 6 (1979), pp. 617–625.
8. Dr. Alfred E. Fischer, "Psychologic Aspects of Pediatrics," *Journal of Pediatrics*, 40 (1952), pp. 254–259.
9. Weiss, pp. 167–168.
10. McDermott, p. 81.
11. Irma Hilton, "Differences in the Behavior of Mothers Toward First- and Later-born Children," *J. of Personality and Social Psychology*, 7, No. 3 (1967), pp. 282–290.
12. Wilson and Edington, p. 103.
13. Charles McArthur, "Personalities of First and Second Children," *Psychiatry*, 19 (1956), pp. 47–54.

REFERENCES FOR CHAPTER 8

1. Douglas Keay, "Margaret Thatcher's Life Story," *Good Housekeeping* (April 1985), pp. 107, 226–228.
2. Gwen Morgan and Arthur Veysey, "The Colonel of Chicago," *Sunday, The Chicago Tribune Magazine*, Section 10 (April 7, 1985), pp. 9–13, 15, and 29.
3. König, p. 58.

REFERENCES FOR CHAPTER 9

1. Stephen Bank and Michael D. Kahn, "Sisterhood-Brotherhood is Powerful: Sibling Sub-Systems and Family Therapy," *Family Process*, 14 (1975), pp. 311–337.
2. Brian Sutton-Smith and B. G. Rosenberg, *The Sibling* (New York: Holt, Rinehart and Winston, Inc., 1970), p. 57.
3. Weiss, p. 129.

4. Lucille K. Forer, *The Birth Order Factor* (New York: David McKay Co., Inc., 1976), p. 67.
5. Richard D. Lyons, "Who's Who . . . and Other First-Borns," *Chicago Tribune*, Tempo Section (February 8, 1979), pp. 1–2.
6. McArthur, pp. 47–54.
7. Weiss, p. 159.
8. Weiss, p. 159.
9. Weiss, p. 160.
10. Alfred Adler, *What Life Should Mean To You* (New York: Capricorn Books, G. P. Putnam's Sons, 1958), pp. 148–149.
11. Nancy Collins, "Funniest Lady," *People Weekly* (April 25, 1983), pp. 91–96.
12. Weiss, p. 154.
13. Weiss, p. 160.
14. Alfred Adler, *Understanding Human Nature* (New York: Fawcett World Library, 1969), pp. 126–127.
15. König, p. 64.

REFERENCES FOR CHAPTER 10

1. Wilson and Edington, p. 94.
2. Norman Lobsenz, "The Middle-Born Muddle," *Family Weekly* (July 24, 1983), p. 2.
3. Weiss, p. 148.
4. Forer, *The Birth Order Factor*, p. 57.
5. Forer, *The Birth Order Factor*, p. 58.
6. Forer, *Birth Order and Life Roles*, pp. 120–121.
7. Wilson and Edington, p. 104.

REFERENCES FOR CHAPTER 11

1. James H. S. Bossard, *The Large Family System* (Philadelphia: University of Pennsylvania Press, 1956), p. 220.

2. König, pp. 76, 81.
3. Jack and Jo Ann Hinckley with Elizabeth Sherrill, *Breaking Points* (Grand Rapids, Mich.: Chosen Books 1985), p. 56.
4. König, p. 77.
5. Peter Richmond, "Weighing the Odds," *Sunday, The Chicago Tribune Magazine*, Section 10 (November 17, 1985), pp. 12, 14, 15, 21, 22, and 24.
6. Frank E. Gaebelein, *The Expositor's Bible Commentary*, Volume 7 (Grand Rapids, Mich.: Regency Reference Library of the Zondervan Publishing House, 1985), p. 171.
7. König, p. 40.
8. Gaebelein, p. 172.

REFERENCES FOR CHAPTER 12

1. König, p. 77.
2. Martin Heerwald, "What Makes Youngsters Laugh?" *Winston-Salem Journal* (June 1, 1980), p. E4.
3. Anne Tyler, *Dinner at the Homesick Restaurant* (New York: Berkley Books, published by arrangement with Alfred A. Knopf, Inc., 1982), p. 32.
4. Sharon Wegscheider-Cruse, *Another Chance* (Palto Alto, Calif.: Science and Behavior Books, Inc., 1981), pp. 128–129.
5. König, p. 80.
6. König, p. 81.
7. Hinckley, p. 66.
8. Dr. Haim Ginott, *Between Parent and Child* (New York: Avon Books, a division of the Hearst Corporation, 1956), p. 69.
9. John E. Gibson, "The All-Important Self-Esteem Factor," *Family Weekly* (June 24, 1984), p. 11.
10. Gordon E. Rowley, "How Birth Order Affects Your Personality," *The Saturday Evening Post* (November 1980), pp. 62, 63, 118.

REFERENCES FOR CHAPTER 13

1. Alfred Adler, *What Life Should Mean to You*, p. 120.
2. Ross Stagner and E. T. Katzoff, "Personality as Related to Birth Order and Family Size," *J. Appl. Psychol.*, 20 (1936), pp. 340–346.
3. Bruce Cushna, Mitchell Greene, and Bill C. F. Snider, "First Born and Last Born Children in a Child Development Clinic," *Journal of Individual Psychology*, 20 (1964), pp. 179–182.
4. Adler, *What Life Should Mean to You*, p. 128.
5. Rudolf Dreikurs, *The Challenge of Parenthood* (New York: Hawthorne Books, Inc., 1958), p. 47.
6. Andrew Henry, "Sibling Structure and Perception of the Disciplinary Role of Parents," *Sociometry*, 20 (1957), pp. 67–74.
7. Wilson and Edington, p. 111.
8. Wilson and Edington, p. 112.
9. Wilson and Edington, p. 112.
10. Amerigo Farina, Herbert Barry, III, and Norman Garmezy, "Birth Order of Recovered and Nonrecovered Schizophrenics," *Archives of General Psychiatry*, 9 (1963), pp. 224–228.
11. Ethel Mary Abernathy, "Further Data on Personality and Family Position," *The Journal of Psychology*, 10 (1940), pp. 303–307.

REFERENCES FOR CHAPTER 14

1. Wilson and Edington, p. 109.
2. Wilson and Edington, p. 110.
3. Norman Miller and Geoffrey Maruyama, "Ordinal Position and Peer Popularity," *J. Pers. Soc. Psychol.*, 33 (February 1976), pp. 123–131.

REFERENCES FOR CHAPTER 15

1. Cecil G. Osborne, *The Art of Learning to Love Yourself* (Grand Rapids, Mich.: Zondervan Publishing House, 1976), p. 33.
2. James T. Baker, "First-Born Sons and Brothers' Keepers," *Christian Century* 95, (Nov. 22, 1978), pp. 1133–1135.
3. Wilson and Edington, p. 119.

REFERENCES FOR CHAPTER 16

1. Barbara Kantrowitz with Nikki Finke Greenberg, "Only But Not Lonely," *Newsweek, On Health* (Fall 1986), pp. 6–7.
2. Kantrowitz, pp. 6–7.
3. David M. Levy, M.D., *Maternal Overprotection* (New York: Columbia University Press, 1943), p. 107.
4. Murray Kappelman, *Raising the Only Child* (New York: The New American Library, Inc., 1975), p. 8.
5. Kappelman, p. 60.
6. Forer, *The Birth Order Factor*, p. 72.
7. Wilson and Edington, p. 29.
8. Wilson and Edington, p. 21.
9. Kappelman, p. 89.
10. John Nisbet, "Family Environment and Intelligence," *Eugenics Review*, 45 (1953), pp. 31–40.
11. Kappelman, p. 66.
12. Forer, *Birth Order and Life Roles*, p. 80.
13. Forer, p. 80.
14. Kappelman, p. 71.
15. Wilson and Edington, p. 19.
16. Meyer Friedman and Ray H. Rosenman, *Type A Behavior and Your Heart* (New York: Alfred A. Knopf, Inc., 1974), p. 9.

17. Ellen Peck, *The Joy of the Only Child* (New York: Delacorte Press, 1977), p. 27.

REFERENCES FOR CHAPTER 17

1. Forer, *The Birth Order Factor*, p. 164.
2. Christopher Drake, "Why an 'Only Child' May Be a Problem Child," *Chicago Tribune*, Lifestyle, Section 12 (November 16, 1980), p. 8.
3. Glenn Collins, "Dad Plays Major Part in Defining a Child's Sex Role," *Chicago Tribune*, Tempo, Section 5 (December 26, 1984), p. 1.
4. Seymour Fisher and Roger P. Greenberg, *The Scientific Credibility of Freud's Theories and Therapy* (New York: Basic Books, 1977), p. 242.
5. Fisher and Greenberg, p. 250.
6. Fisher and Greenberg, p. 251.
7. Maya Pines, "Only Isn't Lonely (Or Spoiled or Selfish)," *Psychology Today* (March 1981), pp. 15, 18–19.
8. W. Peter Blitchington, Ph. D., *Sex Roles and the Christian Family* (Wheaton, Ill.: Tyndale House Publishers, Inc., 1984), p. 76.
9. David M. Levy, M.D., *Maternal Overprotection* (New York: Columbia University Press, 1950), pp. 40, 53, 71, 101.
10. König, p. 29.
11. Kappelman, p. 26.
12. Kappelman, p. 41.
13. Wilson and Edington, p. 17.
14. Wilson and Edington, p. 16.
15. König, p. 26.
16. König, p. 27.
17. Norma E. Cutts & Nicholas Moseley, *The Only Child* (New York: G. P. Putnam's Sons, 1954), p. 120.

REFERENCES FOR CHAPTER 18

1. John P. Jewell, Jr., *The Long Way Home* (Nashville: Thomas Nelson Publishers, 1982).